Meka J.

The ABC's

of Bonding

Strengthening Our Connection with Children

ACKNOWLEDGEMENTS

Editor
Minika Johnson

Cover Illustration
Ramon Roberts

Contributors
DeAndre Boston, Brandon Boston, Kerrie Simon-McMillan
Jennifer Hearn, Jeremy B., Tameka D.
and all the schools/centers, and people I have taught,
worked with, and learn from, and will continue to learn from
as I continue to build and grow

ISBN:979-8-218-03789-5

SPECIAL SALES
Books are available at special discounts for bulk purchases for sales,
promotions or premiums. For more information, visit
www.wedroppinjems.com as our books will be listed on their site. You may also
text book order to 615.854.8486 if you would like to speak with or contact
someone about purchasing the book. Thank you. Make sure to follow
@we_droppin_jems on instagram

Table Of Contents

This book is dedicated to Cortez L. Johnson
You will forever be my shining star.
I am and will forever remain proud of all of your accomplishments,
the work you put in, and obstacles you overcame.
I am so grateful we were able to build in these ways A-Z.
I just wish we had more time to continue to do more,
because even though we did it all, it was SO much more to do.
But for now I will cherish every memory and bond made from our time together.
May your light continue to shine bright as you watch over us in the sky. Until
we meet again...

Love You Cuz

The ABCs of Bonding
Strengthening Our Connection with Children

Preface

Before we get started, let me say this. This book is not for the soft at heart. Nor for people filled with excuses. It's not for the person who cannot be honest with themselves, nor the blamer. This book is also not a "one size fits all" book. We have this saying in education, "If it doesn't apply, let it fly!" Learn what you can from this book and do what you will with the rest. This book is for the person who genuinely wants to be a better teacher, and the person who wants the best for not only their child but for all children! If at any point in this book you hear something that applies to you and your situation, I encourage you to work on it. If something sounds different and interesting to you, I encourage you to try it. Have conversations with other parents, and definitely with your child's teacher about the things you learned and never knew. If you are not here to learn something new, if that's not you, then gone head and go somewhere else. Close this book cause it's about to get real!

This book is real. This is how I really talk, and these are real stories, with real examples. These are real feelings, lessons and expressions as well. Everything talked about in this book is to give you a real understanding. This is how I talk to my friends, employees, parents, and even students when I am putting them up on game. So don't read this book in your professional or academic tone. Read it in your 'I'm sitting down and having honest, fun, and real conversations amongst friends' tone. With that being said, keep in mind the language may get passionate as the south side of Chicago comes out of me at times. What I challenge everyone to do is, really listen and excuse the grammar haha. Now, get ready to open up your heart and mind. Get ready to grasp a better understanding of connecting with your children as you connect with me as well.

Introduction

I feel like my entire life I have been blessed with this gift with children. They have always liked me, wanted to be around me, or play with me. Unless they were my sisters of course (haha). My sisters thought I was lame or at least that's how they made me feel sometimes. Nevertheless, I had a way with them as well. Whether they will admit it or not.

I have always loved children. The tinier they are, my heart goes awwwwwwwww. (I'm not gon' lie though, as they get older my heart starts to go aww). The base relationship though, no matter the age, will always be the same. Children like me, because of my willingness to relate, listen, challenge, and have fun with them. This carries on into teenage years and even adult years. Why is that? Well, I can say it's my God-given gift because it is. Sometimes I just have a way with people. They either really love me or really hate me …well dislike me, (hate is such a strong word) which is fine.
I have no in-between either. Either I like you or I don't. (Adults, that is, it's completely different for children). But for the sake of this book, we are not going to say it's my God-given gift. I want all adults to know, they can be the teacher or person children adore too, because time and time again it has been proven. Not just because you are their parent, provider, caregiver, or even guardian, but because you take the time out on an everyday basis to do the key things that will be discussed in this book. But we'll get to that in a minute.

There will be a level of accountability in this book for every person who works with or has children. Although I do want parents to have a new level of understanding for teachers, this book is for everyone who is caring for a child! Period! Now it is a parent or guardian's job to understand, and hear me when I say this! It's your job to understand that YOU ARE YOUR CHILD'S FIRST, BEST

AND MOST IMPORTANT TEACHER! YOU! YOU! YOU! YOU! Once a parent understands that, things can change. Secondly your home is your child's FIRST AND MOST IMPORTANT CLASSROOM!!!! So, before we get to blaming the school systems, teachers, and educational institutions, ask yourself what are they learning at home? What are YOU teaching them?

Ohhhhhhhweeeeee nah! It's getting hot in here! I told you to close the book if you didn't care. Yes. Yes. Yes. Let's get it crackin! Now that THAT'S out the way, let us understand the role a teacher plays in school. I know you may be wondering, why is she doing all of this? Well, you will see. Because we are all teachers, but do we really understand what it is teachers do!? Or what they have to put up with on a day-to-day basis? Do we understand the training they endure? Why is it important? And why they are so stressed? 'Cause it's never the kids. Well…rarely. Yea? Well, let's get started, shall we?

Teachers in Early Childhood Education or Child Development are required to endure gruesome training repeatedly every year in all regards of play, health, safety, classroom management, child abuse and more. Although I am speaking in reference to childcare centers, most of these training concept requirements, especially the bare minimum, can be applied to all forms of educational school systems. Just a little different sometimes depending on the state and grade. Next, depending on the center or school you teach at, you are forced to abide by their curriculum rules, their center rules, and their philosophy. On top of abiding by state regulations that sometimes don't make sense. And don't let the center be accredited! Oh lawd! Some more rules you have to abide by, that contradicts all the other rules!! Can we say headache? It can either be interesting at times or sometimes a pain in the ass. Yes, I said it. Nonetheless necessary, did I mention the requirements by the state we have to uphold as well? Oh I did? My bad. Curriculums can range from anywhere to a creative curriculum type, to the teachings of Reggia Emilio, Teaching Strategies, Frogstreet with Conscious Discipline, Social and Emotional Learning, (SEL which can be held in all aspects of education, not just Early Childhood) and more. I mean the list is endless, and I'm not going to name all those people or methods. Just know they are out there. Parents and guardians, how many of you study these methods or research those curriculums? I think learning about some of the most popular curriculums can help you. Try looking into them. The only things parents have ever asked me about on their own in regards to schools or specific curriculums are programs based on STEM. (Curriculums strongly based on Science, Engineering, Technology and Math).

Now, I'm not taking anything away from the studies, I've had to repeatedly study or research people like Sigmund Freud, Erik Erikson, Jean Piaget and more. I'm also not taking anything away from the people behind the curriculums and their philosophies. I've had to put their teachings, philosophies and lessons into practice for years. But at this very moment you are about to learn about my methods, philosophies and practices. Not theirs. Remember most of my teachings discussed today will come from, and are stimming from dealing with children of the younger spectrum. And they have been proven in practice as well. Now you may not agree with everything I'm going to say. And that's ok. Hey, I don't agree with all that I have learned from everyone I've had to study in my field. All those curriculums and ideas, philosophies and practices. And that's ok! That's how I was able to develop and create my own process, that has helped me do wonders as a teacher, with things considered impossible by others. Allowing me to be able to tap into my student's full potential while teaching! And I love it! But what I will say is, don't knock it until you try it! I could not say what I didn't agree with, when dealing with children, until I studied and put it to the test. Now I'm asking you to do the same. So stay alert! Feel free to do your own research as well. I'm just here to give you insight from my teachings and point of view. To help you understand what has helped me succeed at being an awesome teacher in general. Because these same methods I use for children, I have used for adults I teach, or train as well. I have already experienced what really does work and what really doesn't work for MYSELF. But something better happened, I implemented what I learned from others, and learned how to make it my own. In which I encourage EVERYONE who is reading this to do. Why, you ask? Because, no two people are the same, and we don't learn the same. Therefore, we aren't going to teach exactly the same either. That's exactly one of the reasons why creative curriculums are my favorite. But I'll explain that later.

Next every teacher has to be CPR and first aid certified. How many parents took first aid class or know how to save their child if they start choking? I personally feel as though it should be a class required by the hospitals FOR FREE for new parents. Just my opinion. We also have hella drills for fires, tornados, shootings, etc. We have to practice once a month to be prepared to get your child to safety in case a fire breaks out, a natural disaster strikes or if someone comes to shoot up the school. Hey Parent's, I was wondering, do you have these drills for your home? The Cosby's did, yea and them smart geeks from the Big Bang Theory as well. The geeks didn't even have children, but I think they had the right idea. I think it's funny how we see these things on TV but never think about implementing them in our homes in real life.

Next, we have to recognize the signs of abuse. Because we, like many individuals who work in the social sector, are mandated by law to report any signs of abuse. Now this conversation can go a whole lotta ways but for the sake of this book we're going to leave it at, how many parents can recognize abuse or signs of abuse? Do you know what they are? In fact, would you even recognize it if you really saw it? Would you know what to do or even know how to begin getting help for your child? For your family? Deep huh? I'mma tell you now, in my humble opinion, most families do not. Because cycles of trauma keep running rapid, especially in our communities. What can we do about it? Oh, we will get to that later.

How are we doing so far? Keeping up? Ok, let's move on. Now I know those 5 paragraphs were a lot to take in, but in summary, what it sounds like to me, teachers' job at school besides teaching is to:

1. Train, study and learn new ways to teach and help the children.
2. Provide a safe environment for them to grow and learn in
3. Be prepared to save their life in emergency situations at all times, no matter the circumstances.
4. Lastly, protect them at ALL COSTS.

Hmmmmm (thinking face). The only thing we not providing is a place to sleep at night… unless it's a 24-hour center. Because they definitely getting fed 3 times a day, and at some centers more. Let's not mention how many pairs of clothing items go home on a daily basis. Hell, I've been saving up clothes for 5 years just for when my center opens, cause' I know it's going to be needed. A lot of centers or even schools, become safe havens for children. I know you're like, where is she going with all this? Rolling your eyes cause' you know, you know. You know where I'm going with this. Parents and Teachers, we want the same thing for the children! We have similar ideologies don't you think? I mean WE both want the same thing! Don't we? Our children to be the best and to succeed. We are BOTH on the SAME TEAM! So why is it always a battle between parents, teachers and administrators? Something has to change. Our responsibilities are very similar when it comes to children at the end of the day. I know how controversial this statement is, and how it may make parents feel. Now let me say, by no means am I being disrespectful towards parents or trying to take what you do on a 24/365-day period in-between times of school away from you. I couldn't even if I wanted to. (The state might be able to tho, too soon? My bad, bad joke). Parents have wayyyyyyyyy more responsibilities than what I've listed, that can effect many things. They also can't leave their children...well shouldn't and aren't encouraged to. I also know the love between a parent and a child is completely different from the love a teacher has for a student. And I know some parents out there will say, "the bond between a parent and a child is unbreakable." But is that really true? Because I have met children and even grown adults that hate their parents. Don't even speak to them. And we can't forget the parents who will say "Well all teacher's aren't good teachers!" "All of them don't care like that!" Yet we can turn that same statement around and hear teachers say "All parents aren't good parents!" "All parents don't care like that!" Because of some of the things they see, and experience while working with children. We can go back and forth all day, because it's some truth to each statement. But that's not what we are here for. I am saying a good teacher and a good parent ARE one in the same simply because they both want what's best for their child/student. And because of that we are on the same team and should act accordingly. I believe this is where that old adage comes from "it takes a village to raise a child", because it simply does. Have you ever seen anyone do it completely alone, with no help whatsoever?

When you drop your child off to me, it's as if I become their assigned "parent" for the assigned time. (Among other things like doctor, magician, counselor, jungle gym, cartoon character, dinosaur and more...the list goes on and on). Teachers and parents we tag teaming like Lita and the Hardy Boys! Or at least supposed to. (What y' all didn't watch the best years of wrestling?!?! It was lit, The Rock, Undertaker, Rikishi!! If you don't know what I'm talking about go look it up on YouTube!) Anyway, I am all of that because it is my responsibility to care, nurture, protect and provide for your child IN YOUR ABSENCE. All within the ramifications of the rules and regulations provided by both the school and YOU the parent. But aparrrreeeeent, a parent is a teacher NO MATTER WHAT. From the time you decided to have children, you signed up for an everlasting job of teaching. Period. Teachers who do not have children can quit teaching anytime they want. A parent cannot, whether you know it or not. Want to admit it or not. You are either directly or indirectly teaching your child or children, forever. So the question then becomes what are you teaching your child?

With that being said, although I do believe everyone is a teacher or becomes a teacher at some point of time; I'm not letting you no good, ignant, good for nothing, I'm just here for a quick dolla ass teachers off the hook! No ma'am, no sir!! Just like we have a notion that there are crappy parents out there, it's definitely some crappy teachers! I see em everyday! If you were once a good teacher and life hit you in a different way, and now you just don't care the same, retire or quit! Do something! But stop teaching. End on a high note. But for you teachers who just don't care… go somewhere! If you are a teacher who has children ask yourself would you want a teacher like yourself? If our jobs are to save, protect, teach and care for the lives we work for every day, would you want a teacher like you caring and teaching your child?

In my mind, I always have to think, what if and plan for the worst possible outcome. Sometimes that could mean giving my life to protect the children. Something I feel that any parent would do for their own children. But the question becomes, parents, would you give your life for a child that's not yours? Hey, teaching ain't for everybody! And due to me seeing some pretty fucked up things with these children, and the treatment they receive from their parents, I'm inclined to say parenting ain't for everybody either. Teachers have to be unselfish, loving, and protective at all costs, while also knowing how to teach. (At least in my field with the babies) Now you older teachers, I would want y'all to be that way, but that theory just isn't consistent with y'all. I don't know, something is a little off. Ha! But hey, I still love and respect y'all tho. The good teachers. Not thecrappy ones. Would a parent who lacks those traits even put their life on the line for their own child? And before you say of course! Really think about it! Then think about some of the people you have encountered, especially children and their parents. Let's not act like there ain't no fucked up parents out here. Would you still say that if you have seen some horrible things? I would encourage you to seriously consider those things as you move through this book. Continue to think, how would I want my child to be treated? Would I want someone doing this to my child? Dare I say, would I even want someone treating me this way? Always think about, consider and fully understand this concept. Because in some areas of the world, when certain teachers work in certain areas, they are sometimes putting their life on the line for your child. It all comes full circle. Honestly, I feel like that for any social sector. People who work for people in general, put their life on the line for others all day, because unfortunately, people are crazy.

Good teachers are able to get through to children by simply being there. Many of the things I talk about are from a child development basis or practice, but work up into adulthood. Whether childcare, elementary, high school, or even college, good teachers are there. They see their students sometimes from 6am to 6pm. Don't let it be an afterschool program or extracurricular activity or sport attached to that time, because then it can become even later. No matter, that GOOD AWESOME TEACHER that your child loves so much is there. And we are going to go over what being there really means and what it looks like. Now that you understand that it's bigger than just teaching, let's enhance your teaching skills. Whether you're a teacher or a parent throughout this reading, REMEMBER WE ARE ON THE SAME TEAM. Parents, Teachers, Care Givers and more get ready to learn your ABCs so you can be "there" strengthening your connection with not only children, but possibly with adults as well. Let's be real, a lot of adults out here acting more childish than their own children. The ABC's of Bonding is to help you Strengthen your connection with children to help **You Both** grow and learn. These practices and methods are what makes me a good teacher. This is how I am able to accomplish so much with my students, or other teacher's students, and it completely stems from my heart. I'm deeply tapped into my inner child, and love it. I truly love children. Children did not ask for you to create them. Children being born comes from the decision of two adults, lying down and having intercourse. With that comes a level of responsibility whether you are ready for it or not. I never understood why people had babies they did not want, or weren't ready to have. I'm not talking to those who wanted them, planned for them, or accepted the responsibility when it arose. This thought process is simply for those who KNEW what they were doing, whether it was to keep a man, trap a woman, not feel depressed or simply just because. Then when that baby arrives, treat them like the scum of the earth, INTENTIONALLY. I, for the life of me, will never be able to understand that. Maybe it is not for me to understand. What I do know is, more parents need to tap into their inner child and remember what it is like to be fearless, curious, and happy, yet easily hurt and confused as a child. Think about your most happiest moments, and then some of your worse moments as a child. Where do the happy memories stem from? Now what are your most unpleasant memories, and how have they shaped your bad thoughts or habits? Now ask yourself this about the bad memories, did you like that feeling? Better yet do you think you deserved to be treated like that? Is it worth passing that same feeling or treatment down to your child? Last but not least, do you even recognize it when it is happening?

Before diving into our ABC's, I want to share something with you that was shared with me while being an Assistant Director of a center. The center had to close abruptly for many purposes, it was old, needed remodeling, but most importantly the state did not like the Director, so they were making her life a living hell and this fell on the center as a whole. Can't say that I cared too much for the Director myself, not that it was right, but I understood why the state was giving her such a hard time. (And when I say state while talking about childcare/school I'm referring to the licensing rep or someone else who is representing the state and can get you shut down, or your child taken from you, for those of you who don't know). Anyway, I was in charge of finding parents a new center/school and helping the staff find new jobs or positions. And this one person who became a close friend who was a wonderful super fantabulous teacher wasn't looking for anything. And I had to ask her, why not, shit you could get a job anywhere! And she said something to me that I felt deep down in my soul. I want to share it with you, and I hope if she ever reads this, she doesn't get mad and understands why I had to share. She said to me, "Girl, I'm over this. I'm tired and I need a break. I'm sick of taking care of other people's kids who don't care. I care more about their child than they do! I'm sick of seeing parents who don't want to get off the phone when they come into the class. I'm sick of seeing them disregard their child when they child is trying to tell them about their day. They up here trying to fight the teachers who are literally watching their child from 6 am to 7 pm because they can't get here to pick them up in time, when they live right across the damn street. Honestly, I'm tired. Did you know (child name) was telling her mom some good news, the mom wasn't listening and told her to shut up talking to her after she started whining. That broke my heart to see. Here I am making all of these accommodations with my son to take care of these mutherfuckas kids and you can't even listen to your child tell you about her good day?! I WISH I COULD UNDERSTAND MY CHILD! I WISH MY CHILD COULD TALK TO ME! I WOULD LOVE TO HEAR HIS VOICE! So, no, fuck this, fuck them, I'mma sit at home, collect unemployment and work with my own damn child. Teach him! Work with him! He needs me! Because the schools I'm sending him to ain't got no good teachers! They don't have a me, and when I need to go back to work cause I need the money, I'll call you up and let you know. Hopefully by that time I can come work for you." And we laughed. I gave her a hug and told her "I completely understand your sentiments and I know it doesn't matter, but I support your decision, and hopefully my business is up and going by then." I felt her, because she WAS going above and beyond. We were working with her, her child did end up coming to the school. And she was stressed, and angry sometimes, because it wasn't easy. Her child was autistic and I love her child to death! He has the biggest and cutest smile, and every time I get a hug or see him and we vibe out, he makes me feel special, cause he don't fuck with everybody haha! I wanted to share that snippet of the story because people say all these things about teachers and act as if teachers are not human too. Like they don't have problems. It's easy for someone to say to me, because I don't have children I don't understand, but that's not true. I don't have to have children to understand what it takes to raise a child, care for a child, nurture a child, spend time with a child, and create a bond with a child. I do it for a living for people who have children. I wanted to share her frustrations, because she is a parent, who teaches. She's a damn good parent, a very strong individual and magnificent teacher! She can be on my team no matter, whenever, however because I've seen the work she put in! I'm so proud of her, and admire her strength! But she is a teacher who nonetheless, shared stories, and has the same sentiments that I am going to share in this book in regards to people and children. As a whole, WE CAN DO BETTER FOR OUR CHILDREN AS A HUMAN RACE, and that is what this book is here to help you do.

While reading this book, I want to encourage everyone to find their specialty in this. Do a SWOT analysis on yourself. (Yes, I'm a business major as well and it's fun combining its tools with education because it is useful). So, as we go through these ABC's, I want you to think about your strengths, weaknesses, opportunities (to be better or think outside the box), and the threats. Threats may be difficult to understand, but think of what can or how you can directly or indirectly cause damage to your child or family. Not just in one way either. Secondly as we go through these ABC's, think holistically! Children don't see color in the form adults do. They are taught that so for all adults reading this, what is going to be required of you is to think outside the box. Get out of your feelings, lean not into your own understanding, and get to understand some new things. Empathize, see things from a different perspective other than your own or what you have been taught. It's time to learn something new. And remember, sometimes it may seem as if I'm talking to parents, but if you are a teacher reading this, I'm talking to you too! Remember this book is for ANYONE working with or around children. Words are interchangeable in this book, remember, because parents are forever teachers. And some of you teachers need to get it together. Although this is aimed to help parents more, remember some of you can be stronger teachers as well. I always look to improve my teaching skills. I encourage you to do so too. Get ready, some hard truths will be spoken, and I want you to LISTEN. Listen with open ears, hearts and minds. It will help you not only with your child but with yourself as well. Yes, I am an African American woman, so a lot of this will be coming directly from my experiences. Remember these are my methods no matter the race, age, creed, culture of my children. When they are in my care, they become my babies. Therefore, everything shared, even some of the hard to hear things would be shared respectfully.

Remember, as I share the breakdowns of why these ABC's are important, some things are for your knowledge and awareness. ALL things are for you to put into practice. Let's get started.

Chapter A

A is for
Awareness, Active, & Attention

Through the years of my experience in teaching. I have noticed time and time again that parents can be fully oblivious or unaware of what's going on. They have no idea what's happening in their child's life. Some even seem not to care at all. They are completely unaware, or seem not wanting to be aware. A lot of times they are completely dismissing their child, more focused on "other things". They don't know that Tommy had a fight at school, nonetheless care to know as to why. They don't know that Sara kicked the winning goal at the soccer game. Even worse they may not know simple things like if their child is right-handed or left-handed. That Michael's favorite color is green and not blue. Just totally unaware! It always amazes me in moments where I talk to parents in general, who have their child inside a school or center, and they have NO IDEA what's going on. They don't even know their child's teacher's name. This has happened to me several times in asking parents who are leaving their INFANTS with teachers. HOW?!? How don't you know that teachers name?! How do you not know the name of the person you are leaving your infant with?!?! When parents are unaware. It usually leads to issues with their children. The biggest one is acting out for attention.

That brings us to our second word. Yes. Attention. You have to be AWARE and pay ATTENTION, not only to things involving your children, but to your children themselves. If you don't, more than likely your child will start to act out, to get your attention. It can start minor at first, and if not addressed properly (whoa another A word, that one's free), it can grow bigger and lead to insecurities, behavior issues, self-esteem issues and more. Typically, when children act out,it's for a reason. If you are aware of what's going on in your child's life, it can be a little bit easier to figure out if they are acting out for attention. Then, what type of attention are they seeking? Is it love, time, support? It can be a billion things, but what? You will only know if you are staying ALERT (another free A word), AWARE and are paying ATTENTION to them. Are you giving your child the attention they need?

Lastly, keep your child active. Activity is important! "An idle mind is the devil's playground", you've heard the saying. You have to keep them busy! Being active will coincide with other letters in the alphabet as well. So pay attention as we move along. Staying active can be beneficial for you and your child. It helps them stay fit, healthy and don't forget it helps burn out that energy so you can get some sleep. Children play, move, hop, jump, skip, run and explore all day. They are doing what they are supposed to do, and you get mad!? Instead of getting mad, you should be getting active with them. And let me say this, it is more than one way to keep your child active, without you having to run around like a chicken with your head cut off. We will discuss those ways as we go through the rest of our ABC's. Remember to always be aware of what your children are doing. Pay attention to them and give them the attention they need or else they will act out for attention. It doesn't always have to come from you. They will end up getting someone's attention, and depending on who, it can turn out to be dangerous. Continue to stay active in your child's life and keep them active. It's important! I always tell people, "When I'm not busy, that's when I get in the most trouble. I do things that I'm not supposed to do that I wouldn't be doing if I stayed active." It's the same thing for your child when they get bored. Guess what, when boredom strikes, they are going to go find something to get into no matter the age. So stay alert. Be proactive instead of reactive.

Chapter B

B is for
Balance, Battles & Boundaries

You have to find balance with everything I'm mentioning throughout this ENTIRE book. You are going to have to know when to pick your battles. And to set boundaries, also known as rules for your classroom, home, and self. All of these work hand and hand. Even as I write this, I'm trying to find the best way to explain it, so that it's understood and done correctly. I honestly believe there's no one way to explain or do this, it only has to be done. So let me give examples. Try to follow me.

You know how you have to maintain a home and work life balance? Well, you have to maintain a child and teacher/parent balance. See teachers and the school have to be whatever is needed sometimes. We may sometimes be a doctor, counselor, judge, rocketship, jungle gym, dinosaur, then back to being called mom accidentally on purpose. What I'm saying is we wear many hats. And have to wear those hats at the right time. Giving each student in our class the proper attention they need. That can sometimes be more than 20 students. When I worked at CPS (Chicago public schools) I was in a class of 45 kindergarteners, at one time. Yea. Say it slow...forty-five. All three kindergarten classrooms had 45 children in them, and they still had the audacity to try and keep enrolling more. Crazy right? With no teachers assistants for any of the Kindergartener teachers. I ended up having to rotate between those classes at the time...amongst a billion other things at that school. Anyway, some of you can't handle 5 of your own children, or the one you have, let alone 45 of them that are not yours. How do we do this? Balance. We choose our battles and set our boundaries. It sounds a little like this.

"Ok class can you tell me some of the rules we have and why?" Let them speak. See what they know and don't know. Then continue. "Ok. Great, now I have some more important rules or things you missed that need to be added on." You then say what they are. You are setting your tone and boundaries. Continue to ask them questions, suggestions, and opinions of what else they think is needed and why. Let them share (balance). Let their voice be heard, get to know them and hear what they may say. Some things may totally surprise you! Let them set their own boundaries as well. This is done a lot with younger children, but what does it look like for older children? "Hey ma, can I go over Jason's crib?" "Yea, but be back before the street lights on." "Why? They come on at 7pm, by the time I get there Imma have to leave!" "Why do you think I want you home by 7pm?" Let them answer. Then ask, "what would you have me do if I was in your shoes?" Let them answer. Balance. Discuss, maybe even compromise, but what comes out of the conversation? A level of understanding of each other's boundaries. Boundaries are not just about personal space. It is also about respect as well. Discussing the ins and outs, and the reasoning behind them, you may have just saved yourselves a battle. Or maybe picked one up hahaha. But no matter what, the discussion is necessary!

Amongst other things to balance, you have to balance your time, efforts, attention, your downtime for you, and them, I mean you have to balance it all! If not, you will have battles every single day and it will be about every single thing! And that will become frustrating. For instance, the number one reason parents do not want to take their children to the grocery store is because why? Because they don't want the tantrums and questions of can I have this or that and their child falling out in public. But what if, what if you set proper boundaries before you went in and before you left home?

Then reviewed those boundaries again before you went into the store? Let them know "hey, if you do this, (give example) you won't be able to come with me next time." And when they do mess up, stick to your guns (don't let them go the next time), but also give them another chance to learn (offer another chance later). Repeating the boundaries every time, it's done until they get the message? And you do this for every aspect, for every tone you want to set.

You have me time every Saturday in your mancave from noon to 2pm. If you repeatedly do that and go over the rules, they will LEARN not to disturb you on Saturday from noon – 2pm (of course unless it's an emergency). If you have me time every Sunday in your she shed the same rules apply. But remember if and when you set time for yourself you do the same thing for your family and your children together and individually. Balance. You are also setting a routine. But we will get to that later.

This same concept applies to teachers. And a good teacher will know how to do this well. It is very easy for a teacher to do all of this with a child they like. But what about a child that gives them the hardest time? They tend to make their battles harder by not giving them the same boundaries or not knowing when or how to pick their battles. They don't balance their time with that child because they would prefer to not deal with them at all when they should actually work with them more. Yes, let me say that again. Sometimes when you are dealing with a particular student you don't want to deal with their behavior, but you should actually work with that behavior child more. Picking your battles and setting your boundaries and creating balance in your classroom may sometimes mean having to deal with that child more. And a lot of times, teachers do the exact opposite and that's why that child creates problems for their class. Sometimes BALANCE does not mean equally when it comes to children. It means necessary! And it is our job as adults to do, see, notice and balance out what is necessary to be done or get done for our children, whether it's 2 of them or 45. Every battle with your child is not meant for you to give into or compromise on. Some battles you have to tough it out and stand your ground on. I cannot tell you which, because I don't know what tone you want to set for your home or in which ways you guide your children to be. All I can do is use examples from me and my class. So, I'll give you brief examples.

In my class, I don't condone disrespect, but I also know children will be children. I let them know that it is rude and disrespectful to interrupt each other when we are taking turns (keyword taking turns) talking and letting each other know how our day went. They are not to interrupt. It is rude and disrespectful to hit each other or call each other names. It is also rude and disrespectful to tease or be a sore loser, or winner. In a world where they are putting up so many false narratives for children, I refuse to do so. When I see any of those actions, I correct them immediately so they know not to do it again. Sometimes in that correction, I am picking a battle because sometimes it can get ugly before it gets better. But that is my choice. In the same token, it's a balance mechanism to all of this. For example, when we are sitting and taking turns talking because they are children, I understand they can't sit still for long periods of time. As long as they are not hurting or interrupting anyone or making loud quiet noises, I let them move around on the carpet. A battle I choose to ignore. When we are playing and they say something like "Ms. J you're a slowpoke" or tease me, I don't correct it. When they do it to each other, after doing it to me, I listen to see what comes out of it. Sometimes it's a conversation, or a lesson of understanding why we don't talk like that. Or I choose to ignore it and let them figure it out on their own. I'm letting them choose their battles. If I have a child who constantly gets in trouble for hitting, and one day a child chooses to hit that child back, I choose to turn the other cheek. I don't reprimand the child who defended themselves finally. Sometimes I may even be a little proud. Because although I don't condone violence, I do believe in speaking up for yourself and defending yourself. And let's face it, it is all needed. That child has chosen their battle. I guide them through it, when the conversation is needed. When we are playing a game, maybe the children are going down the slide head first. I choose to pick my battle and let them slide head first if they are being safe and I can monitor them. No need to ruin their fun. If we are playing a game and it deems a winner, the loser does not get to stomp and pout. You congratulate them and try harder next time. I see nothing wrong with a little friendly competition, especially since the world is set up that way. Through this I teach the children how to work better together, and to clap for one another. It pushes them to want to be better. The tone that is set for my classroom overall is a free thinking, yet respectful tone. I have my time, they have their time, then we have our time together and separately. Those are tiny examples of how I choose to balance out my class, pick my battles and set boundaries. In that, WE ALL get to choose our battles and learn that, there are consequences and repercussions for our choices. I hope these examples helped you better under BALANCE, BATTLES and BOUNDARIES. With that being said, let's move on to the letter C.

Chapter C

C *is for*
Challenge, Choices, Correct, Creative & Communicate Candidly

Some things mentioned in B will be mentioned here as well. As I said before, everything is tied together. C is for challenge, choices, correct, creative and communicate candidly. It sounds like a lot doesn't it? It's really not, especially if done every day from the time your child arrives. Communication is key. If you don't know anything about me, know that. So, let's start there. Communicate candidly. What does that mean? Sometimes as parents and teachers or as the world as a whole, we censor our children. We take their voice away. They are not allowed to speak for themselves, express themselves, let alone think for themselves. Then we wonder why they do the things they do, or act the way they act. It is because we censor them too much. They have no chance of learning who they are because they are too busy being who YOU feel they should be. Not who they want to be. So, when they grow up and are no longer under your house or wing, they lose it. Because you never talked to them, communicated with them, you have no idea how they feel. Or worse when they have their outbursts, you call it a tantrum and dismiss it, when sometimes it is a sincere cry for help. Sometimes you censor them even when they do talk. So, the question is, how can we change this. It's simple, let them talk!!!

When you are having candid conversations, it is to listen with intent! I am a teacher. I can't help but to listen to everyone with "teacher's ears" lol. I have adults who come and open up to me out of nowhere. Sometimes even after meeting them 5 minutes ago. It's crazy! I used to be scared when adults did it, "I just met you, why are you telling me all your business", was what I was thinking.

22

Y'all it used to really weird me out. But every one of them always said they feel better after talking to me, and that I am a great listener and give good advice. I just be there for them how I would want someone to be there for me if I was in need. That's all I'm doing when talking to people who approach me out of nowhere. (People used to say when they would finally have a conversation with me, "O you real down to earth," and I would be like, "What you thought I was?" And they would be like "Stuck up." (Ha!) I'm often left wondering, how did it work out for them, or did they even take the advice. Overall, what that has taught me is, as much as our youth needs it, adults need it too. Everyone just wants to be heard and feel like their voice matters. So we have to learn how to talk to one another, and hear each other out. When you do that, you will be so surprised at how much you can learn! Now I know it can be a bit tricky for parents to have candid moments with their children, because if they truly get to express themselves you may deem it as disrespect. Therefore, I challenge all parents to make a routine of scheduling candid conversations. You can approach the situation like a teacher. I found it to be a good way to gain student's respect. Not gonna lie, the older they are, the harder it is to gain their respect. It's like you have to earn it, and by earning it, you always have to show them you ain't the one. Or you are the one...And for those who don't know what that means, it means you ain't scared. Let's go! It's like that part in Sister Act, where ol' boy was like, "Hey I think Sister Mary Clarence is a Sista Sista" you feel me? The only reason they were giving her such a hard time is because they were trying to make her crack and leave. They thought she was just another teacher who didn't care, and they wanted her out, or just wanted to be able to fly through what they called the bird course. But she rose to the challenge. (Can y'all tell that's my movie?) Either way, you are not to be walked over.

23

Anyway, back to what I was saying, approach the situation like a teacher. What does that mean? Well for one, the student has to feel safe and comfortable talking to me. In parent language, especially for some of you parents, more than others, feeling safe to talk means "I'm not gonna get my ass whooped if I say this, right?" A lot of times it flows naturally, I'm usually the one to notice something is wrong. I start the conversation but I don't force it. Does that make sense? The conversation has to flow, feel natural. For younger children it may go like this "Hey Brooke Brooke, what's the matter?" "Why are you pouting?" She will either let me know or turn away. If she turns away, I'll say "OK, I'll let you pout in silence". She will come back to me when she is ready. When she does come back to me, sometimes her mood is changed or it's the same. Either way I ask the question again. She answers and the conversation starts from there. Me letting her walk away without getting upset, yelling at her, or being petty, lets her know it's safe. So when she does come back again to talk, the next time it won't be so hard.

Older children are different. One they don't talk because they feel like everything will be used against them in the court of law. Meaning if they honestly told you how they feel or felt, or something you wanted to know, they would get in trouble. Put on punishment, grounded, and or beat. And most of the time I have seen this to be true. That's why a lot of students feel like they can talk to their teacher or a coach or someone else they trust, before talking to their parents. That's why it's important to communicate with your child's teacher. A good teacher will be able to relay these things back to you as the parent, so everyone involved can be on the same page. But trust has to remain all the way around, it has to be some level of discretion when doing this. If a student found out a teacher was telling their parents everything…they will no longer talk to that teacher…and that can knock out one of your lines of knowing what's going on. That child can stop opening up to that teacher, the same way they have stopped opening up to you. On the same token, if the teacher feels like the child's home is in no way, shape, form or fashion a safe place, they aren't telling those parents anything. The school is a safe haven. The teacher is working on ways to help that child, without the parents being involved. It can become complicated real quick. You see how battles and balance can come into play here.

So how do we communicate candidly with older children, and make them feel safe to speak? What do these conversations look like with older students? Simply pure, raw and unfiltered. Yes a lot of times these students are cursing. I'm not going to stop them in the middle of cursing because I deem it as disrespect. I have to remove my feelings from the situation and listen with intent. What is the ground breaking problem? That is what I am listening for. How are these conversations started? Believe it or not, most of the time they come to me, the teacher, because that relationship is built. But in cases where you have to get it out of them, I may start the conversation saying something like this, "Hey wassup, I noticed you were off yo' game today, that's not like you, what's going on?" Sometimes it's not that simple, and I have to open up and be vulnerable first. They then feel safe, open up and tell me what's going on. What does that mean? That means I share a piece of information about myself that I know, they don't know, in hopes that they open up and let me know what's going on. If we don't talk about it right there in that moment, they come back later, when they are ready to share. Because of my bond with that student, I usually learn what's bothering them right away.

I want to point out how sometimes I have to open up and share personal instances about myself to my students. I don't think parents understand just how powerful this is. I mean children naturally have this preconceived notion about their parents. So preconceived, that when you tell them a little about your life before they were conceived it changes things. I'm not a parent, but when I tell my students the smallest of something, especially if it is related to something they like, it blows their mind. I tell them I used to cheer, I can do splits, I can dance, they go crazy! Can't believe it! If I tell the babies I used to watch power rangers and I was the yellow ranger growing up, they can't believe it! They start laughing and asking a whole bunch of questions to see if it's true. Through this we are creating stronger bonds. I am becoming relatable, it's easier for them to approach me. When talking to high schoolers, it gets a little more real. I say from 6th grade on up actually because this is when life starts to happen differently for these students. There are more avenues of trouble purposely put in their face. They have more responsibilities, willingly and unwillingly sometimes. They start to get in trouble more, they have questions, they are being tested, going through peer pressure and numerous things. The number one thought in a child's mind during these moments, is you don't understand. Because of that, they are afraid to share with you some of the things they might be going through. Extend yourself first. Because we all know that nobody's perfect, and we have all done some things. As adults we're so busy trying to keep the children from those same experiences, that we don't even recognize when the world is exposing itself to our children first. So share. I have real ass conversations with children of all ages. Words change based upon age. For my highs choolers who're getting into fights, they can never imagine me fighting. I don't like to, but I have been in fights with both men and women. I share what lessons came from that. I remember one time I shared with a group of students that I slashed a girl's tires in college and was gonna keep slashing them until I got my money she owed me, because she was tryna play me. I told that girl that too, since our mutual friends at the time "didn't" want us fighting. (Rolls eyes, they were good body guards, I mean friends, walked with her all the time). She ended up transferring schools. I also ended up explaining why I did it, so they can understand some things, based upon whatever we were talking about at the time. Which more than likely was don't underestimate people, especially quiet ones, because you never know what people are going through. One, they were shocked, two they understood the message. I'm shortening the whole story up for the sake of the book, but it's always a shock factor to children because sometimes, some people just "look" like they haven't done anything ever right? I be telling the kiddos "can't judge a book by it's cover". I tried weed because in high school I wanted to see what the hype was about, and I wasn't impressed. Had my first drink at the age of 12. And guess what, I'm sure my parents never knew this until now. Ironically for that same reason the children think that it can't be possible, "I'm a goody two shoes", right? HA! I share these stories and it opens up the floor for a candid conversation, with no judgment. It allows them to feel comfortable with me to share, and in return I know how to talk to them and get through to them if something needs to change in their life. Why is this so important? When I do this, I show them that I'm not perfect, wasn't perfect and once was at a point in my life where I experienced the same pressures and curiosities as them. I can help them get through whatever they are going through, but only if they let me. Parents, you have to understand the power in this too. If they look up to you, it is easier to convey that message. We are so focused on keeping them away from the truth and this and that, not realizing sometimes, it's going to catch up to them anyway. Help them be more prepared for it so they don't repeat the same mistakes, or make new ones that are even worse. Furthermore, for teachers, know these students background, where they came from. Understanding their background can help you be more relatable and or empathetic. Notice I said empathetic and not sympathetic. None of these students want your sympathy! They just want to be understood!

That's where a lot of teachers fail, feeling sorry for them. Never do that! That's how you play yourself, because these students are smart! Their circumstances don't make them stupid or unworthy, it just puts them behind a little. When dealing with these types of students, the best rule of thumb is to imagine yourself in their shoes. Then ask yourself how would it make you feel? After asking yourself that and answering your own question, continue to ask yourself, what would you want someone to do for you? I'm quite sure the answer wouldn't be to feel sorry for you! Whatever that answer is, proceed to do that, for that child. It's these types of ordeals that shows why having candid conversations is extremely important.

Help them learn to make a choice. Help them to understand that ALL choices have consequences and repercussions. Repercussions could either be bad or they can be good. Start giving them options at a young age (something that we will discuss more later). Make sure they are options you will be ok with, no matter which they choose and go from there. This teaches them to make their own decision, understand the consequences of the decision and make them feel like they have some control. I mean think about it really. Have you ever met an adult that literally has the hardest time making a decision? I don't know about you, but it drives me crazy. It is also a critical thinking skill, teaching them how to think for themselves as well. You also have to remember this trick, which is not to give in and or back down on your part. When they make a choice, you as the adult have to tough it out as well. So many times the adult gives in because they are scared, they don't like the choice the child made or simply they don't want to hear them cry, or worse allow them to learn. We either give in or make the decision for them, taking the choice away all together and it doesn't help. Allow them to make their choice and follow through. Doing this will help you guide them into the direction you want them to go until they are able to make their own decisions completely on their own. Make sure you watch them as they start to make their own choices as they start to grow and get older. This will tell you so much about your child.

Get Creative. No one likes a boring teacher. Name a thing you learned from a boring teacher. I'll wait. That's right, nothing! But I bet you can name a whole bunch of things you learned from a teacher who was creative and made learning fun. You have to be creative and think outside the box. Every moment is a learning moment. It's all about the way you choose to go about it! Make learning interesting, make spending time creative. And they will never forget those moments. I can testify to creativity with teachings done with me as a child. Something as simple as getting a super long yellow notepad and telling me to write out books. For each page I filled on a yellow notepad, I would receive a dollar. As a child I thought that was a no brainer! Easy money! I didn't realize what my grandmother was doing at the time, it didn't hit me until I became a teacher myself! Through this creative summer notion my grandma was having me do, I was practicing reading, writing and math all at the same time. Not only that, critical thinking and decision making skills, because she never forced us (me and my sisters) to do it. It was an option. It was in my power to figure out how much money I wanted because I knew I got a dollar for each page I filled. I had to put in work though, filling those yellow notepads took a lot! You know how many pages from a book I had to write down to fill that page to receive a dollar?!? That also taught me the importance of work ethic! That's creativity! It wasn't fun for me, but it was memorable. I'm sure it was fun for my grandma though. It wasn't until I got older I understood all those little laughs she did every time she would walk past and see me writing away. Entrepreneurship has always been in me, teaching too. My grandma was able to recognize it in me from an early age and got creative with my teachings and work ethic over the summer. Oh how I wish I would have understood and known these things about her before she passed away. It's so many things I could have learned from her. She died my sophomore year in college, the same year I picked up my child development degree causing me to double major. I was going to school for business originally. I never wanted to work for anyone, and I loved art and children. I knew that I didn't have to have a degree in child development to own a school, but a smooth cursing out from the dean of family and consumer science changed all of that (hahaha) and I'm so grateful for it. Art was my first love, but art schools were super expensive. I ended up learning that I could combine my love of children and art in childcare, when I was volunteering at the school campus. It was not until the funeral did I learn that she herself owned a school on 71st street on Chicago's south side. I wanted to own my own childcare center and never knew anything about this. I could just imagine all of the creative stuff I could have learned from her and business aspects too. The point of this story is to show how creativity can work, and it may not hit them right then and there. The child may be thinking a whole different way, while you as the adult can have another intention for them, that will give them an aha moment later. Creativity also doesn't always have to mean fun, but it does always have to mean interesting. This strenuous ordeal was not fun for me, but it piqued my interest enough to do it. My grandma though, she had the fun! Creativity doesn't only have to be fun for the child, I would highly suggest it be fun for you as well.

Challenge! We go wrong here so often. Your child or student is not bad. They are bored! You are not challenging them enough, or you are not challenging them the right way. A healthy push is good. When you do that, you encourage them to get out of their comfort zone. You challenge them to see how far they can get before they break. You observe this and it shows you at what pace to move forward with them when you are challenging them. When this is done correctly, you are improving self esteem. It shows the child that they can do it!! That no obstacle is too big. It can show them that they are indeed smart and determined as well. Challenging them can also show how much you care. Just make sure that when you are doing this, you are doing it in a healthy and balanced way. Don't push them so hard that they shut down. We don't want that. That happens too often. Do it in a way that it's barely noticeable. When you do this, it's done with a lot of patience, encouragement and love. For example, let me share a story.

One year while working for a Chicago Public School, I was put on a certain student as "punishment", because of me sharing my feelings of being over qualified to conduct recess for the whole school. In other words I wanted to continue to help the students learnand assist the teachers in these ordeals, because a lot of them were struggling. I was originally hired to help the 1st grade teachers get their low students back on track, adding additional support by working with them during certain class sessions. Majority of the students were way below grade level in areas of reading, some were low in the areas of math. I rotated between 3 first grade classrooms. Well the next year all that changed. I was then put on recess for the entire school's k-8th grades. We were supposed to rotate between TA's and ESP's (Education Support Personnel, but it was just a fancy word for security in my opinion). At least that's what I was told. So that I could continue to have a schedule in which I could continue to work with the lower level students. Well, you know how that goes, the admin says one thing then does another. Not only was I conducting recess with two other counterparts, but I was often pulled to sub classes when subs called in, teachers called in or when teachers left early. Although I was building relationships with children in the entire school, I hated doing recess because I felt like my credentials were going to waste. This is not what I signed up for, so I decided to speak up. Well they put me on this second grade student who I was familiar with from first grade, but didn't have many chances to work with due to absences. This is what I was told verbatim, because I will never forget. "Ms. Johnson, due to your insistence on working with lower level students and putting your credentials and experience to use, we are putting you on a one on one assignment with (said child). You can do whatever you want with (said child), just keep the child under control and out of the teacher's way". "The child will be back next week and in Ms. (said teacher) class". You can go and talk to the teacher if you want, observe the class and see if it's anything else the teacher needs". I said "okaaayyy" in the most confusing manner and went to the class. I talked to the teacher and asked if there is anything I should know about the child. Teacher says "No, here's the child seat, but I'd prefer you to work with the child in the back", pointing to a little table in the back corner. Then continues to say "After the child gets in, whenever the child acts up, it would be best if you remove the child from class, because I don't want the child distracting the class and throwing me behind in my lessons you know". I'm like "yeah ok".

So of course by now you know I'm wondering what the hell is going on? Then I met the student. First thing I noticed is, the child definitely needed to be in a special needs class. I'm wondering why the child isn't and why ain't no helping to do so, so I start asking questions. OMG why did I do that? Do y'all know what staff and other teachers start telling me? They said to forget about the child, the child was nothing, the mother wasn't shit, older sibling wasn't shit, and to just forget about helping. Y'all I could not believe my ears. Now I'm mad! So I started doing some investigating to find out what was required to get the child into a special needs class. The requirements for that were even crazier!! The child was required to do 2 tier programs that could be done either before or after school. Could not miss a certain amount of days from school, or couldn't be suspended a certain amount of times. The mom had to put in a request specifying that she wanted her child to be reviewed for SPED. Could not miss not one SPED meeting, and some more ridiculous shit. Now I know some of you may be like why is this crazy? Well the mom was a single parent, working, the child had epilepsy and had a series of seizures all the time, so chances of missing school is high. Due to this medical condition the child had behavioral issues. The rules were set up against a child that APPARENTLY needed the help!! But let's continue, me being me, had to do something, so I talked to the mom in secret. Told her to not tell the school I was in communication with her, and we were going to work together to get her child in SPED.

Now the child wasn't book smart, but was definitely street smart! Had a lot of common sense. What messed with the child's self-esteem was their inability to do what their classmates were doing. This is what caused the behavior issue as well. No one wanted to work with the child, not even the teacher. How would that make you feel? In second grade, don't know what an A looks like, can't count to 10, can't even spell their own name? This broke my heart y'all cause I teach this to two year olds!!! And here I am working with a child who's 8 years old, and knows none of this!! Imagine how I felt knowing someone who was 8 could not do what some of my 2 year old's could. Not because the child didn't want to know, but because no one was willing to teach them! No one was willing to challenge themselves to do what was right for that child! Until I came along. I had to tell the mom straight up like this "This school don't give a fuck about your child, but I do, but you gone have to work with me on this, or it ain't gone work". I had to tell the parent "I'm on the school's radar, they don't like me cause I ask questions and imma bout to get to work". Gave her my cell phone number and that's how we stayed in communication. First thing first, request a SPED review. We put our plan into place and got to work.

Now that I gave you the back story, understand, before we continue, this is how I challenge all my students, no matter the age. I also make it my purpose to challenge myself. I share this story a lot because this was not only one of my biggest challenges, but one of my biggest accomplishments with any student I have ever worked with. Because sometimes when children are this old and this far behind, it's almost impossible to get them to care enough to WANT to learn. And we all know you can't help no one who doesn't want to help themselves. To get the child into SPED was going to be a challenge, but not like the one faced working with the child. I came home everyday with welts on my arm from restraining the child, to keep them from hurting themselves. Everyday was a fight, if not with the child, with the admin or the teacher of the classroom. I had to continuously remind the parent when I was going to be out, so that she wouldn't send her child to school when I wasn't there. Because if she did, they were going to suspend them, and on days the parent didn't listen, that is exactly what happened. It was a very rocky beginning, with the flipping of a desk, tearing papers off the boards, slapping students, pulling out hair and shutting down. But what I had to show the child first was that I wasn't backing down. Because the first instinct for that child was I didn't care anyway. What made me different from the others? And I'm sure mom felt that way too. But I had to show them. I had to show I cared. Even if and when the child was acting crazy. After realizing I wasn't backing down and I do care, it wasn't until then, when I was allowed to help.

Keyword here is allowed. The child allowed me in, with baby steps of course. Not fully trusting, but trusting enough to see what I would do and how I could help. From there it grew daily. In the midst, the child would often have moments of shutting down. Since I had to document everything for SPED anyway, I started noticing the patterns. The shutting down part always arrived when learning something new, or when the other students in the class were being click-ish. So the first thing I did to improve the social aspect was take the child to the other 2nd grade class that had more behavior issues and students on a lower level. This helped my student and that 2nd grade teacher, because I was able to do the classroom management so the teacher can teach her class. This allowed my student to be involved in class participation. This also allowed me to work with my student in group settings, while helping other students that were behind as well. I honestly would have rather been in that class with my student permanently. (I know right, y'all like, you wanted to be in the problem class? Yes! cause when I was there there weren't any problems. About 30 Black children in a class with behavior problems with a white teacher who couldn't manage the class. No learning was going on at all when I wasn't there) It made more sense…but you know how that goes, it would be too much like right. I was practicing inclusion in this class because my student's teacher was not doing that for them. Keep the child out of the way, remember? So that's what I did. It's funny how when the student is doing better in another teacher's class, how all the sudden that student has to be in their class only. It's also funny how all of a sudden, it's because their teacher, now suddenly wants to be involved. Yea, all that "Ms. Johnson you can do whatever, however, just keep the child out the way" went right out the window, when the child is starting to show slight progress. So now we are back in the child's normal class. I'm mad, the other teacher is sad, and that other class went back to being a mess with ESP's and security being called to the room every 5 minutes.

The teacher wanted us to go back to our corner in the back. Well ugh, no! My student is going to sit at their desk, and participate with the class, and with group settings with you until they are ready to come and sit back here with me. This was not as effective in the child's regular class as it was effective in the other class because of the teacher. So for the most part, the student came to the back with me and we worked. I encouraged the child more, as I started to challenge them more. I always would say give me one more, to push them just a little further, but not enough to make them shut down. That grew into, give me one more and we will stop, or take a break. And they did, and I stayed a woman of my word. That number would slowly increase to 2 more, 3 more, before we take a break and they would do their part. It came to a point that they would slowly start to push them self more saying to me "ok Ms. Johnson, one more". Then that grew into choice, "do you want to do one more or two more?" And with everything we did, that's how I approached it. Saying "you can do it!" "There you go!!" "Yes!" "Who's Smart?!" I would sit there and wait for a reply, and sometimes even a little dance, constantly saying to this child "you got this!" With this technique I got the child to want to learn more, do more and even participate with the class more as well. And with that came opportunities for progress, but more challenges as well!

Now mind you I was teaching this child how to write, letter and number recognition, how to spell their name, regular sight words and sight word reading books, in a tiny corner in the back of the room away from the "teacher". I had to constantly work on this child's attitude, social and emotional development, their confidence which was the biggest challenge, because the child had to believe in themselves. Also teach the child how to use a computer, raise hand, stand in line, and increase the leadership skills this child had in their own right, because they were there. I was not considered a "teacher" not because I didn't have the degree, but because I didn't have an extra sheet of paper called a certificate that cost more money. Money that I thought I had spent to get the Degree, that I had gone to school for, that should have already qualified me for a teaching position…but that's another conversation for another book. Nor was I considered an IEP (individual education personnel), which is what the child needed. On paper just considered a TA, but to that child, it grew into me becoming their teacher and not the teacher they actually had. Eventually with all the success we were having, the student regained confidence to want to join in and be a part of the class. With the child wanting to be a part of the class more, I had to grant that child's wish, but the child also had to prove to me that they could handle it. I had to grant that child their independence.

In those moments of participating in class, the child would notice how far behind they were and come back to the back of the class with their head hanging low. We would talk and I would challenge that child not to give in so easily. I would remind them that they are doing good, and show them how far they have come from not giving up. I also had to remind that child that I had their back. And you know there came a time where I had to deliver on my word intentionally and the reason why angered me so much, because of how hard the child was working and how far they had come. So y'all know I don't play about my babies, and at this point in time, like so many others, I had to go there with the teacher.

One day the child is participating with the class as a whole, meaning they are participating with the other teacher. I'm simply observing and encouraging my student. By this time, I have built relationships with the entire class and encouraged them to encourage this student and be patient with them as well. So essentially the class is rooting for the child when they are all together as a student body as well. That means, that not only does my student want to be treated like all of the other students in the class, they should without a matter of doubt, and the student body wants to see it too. Well on this day, my student had shown me that all those pep talks about raising your hand to answer the question had sunk in, and put it into practice. I watch from the back, observing every single thing. The teacher asks a question, the child raises their hand to answer the question. They were extremely excited in fact and I can see them mumbling the correct answer to themselves over and over again. I see the teacher purposely call over the child to children who have their hands raised, even calling some of them twice. Not calling my student at all. I'm thinking to myself, really?!?! Well, I guess the child was thinking the same thing because when the teacher moves on to the next subject the child loses it. For the first time in a long time the child snaps, pulling papers off the board, flipping desks and chairs over, screaming and yelling. The teacher looks at me, like get the student, and I'm looking back at the teacher like nope. I let the child flip over a couple of more desks, and pull some more papers off the board, before calling the child's name. I was just happy I didn't have to stop the child from slapping a student hahaha. But I call the child's name and the child immediately stops and starts crying. I go give the child a hug, and say let's go for a walk, the teacher looks and says to me as we head out the door, "you not gone clean this up", and I politely say "no." I grab the child's hand, and before leaving I say calmly to the teacher as she looks at me in disbelief, I say "don't you have a degree as a teacher? Didn't you take a special needs class? You purposely called everyone else with their hands up, except this child, knowing they are trying to fit in. You caused this, you clean it up, I need to calm this child down." And then we walk out of class and stayed out of the class. What that moment did was show that Ms. Johnson did indeed have their back, and indeed saw what was going on. We had a conversation and I told the child that I understood how they felt and why they did what they did, and even though I let it ride this time, I would not be able to do so again. I wanted that child to be better. I also explained to the student that me allowing them to ransack the class was more for teaching the teacher a lesson. (example of a candid conversation) We talked, and the child let me know how they felt, and how the teacher made them feel. This made our bond stronger because the child was able to see that Ms. Johnson truly did have their back. After having a great candid conversation and a level of understanding we went back to class and worked in our little corner in the back. Now you know I was in total surprise of seeing it happen again after the child had worked up enough courage to participate with the class in a shorter time frame.

Yes! That's right. Excuse my French, but that dumb ass teacher had the audacity to let it happen again. But to my surprise the child's response was not the same. It was so different that it BROKE my heart. I watched that child hold their hand up for 2 minutes straight, at this point I'm timing it. And when the teacher did not call on this child, the child did not scream. The child did not flip a desk over. The child did not pull a piece of paper off the wall, none of that. The child simply sits at the desk and starts to cry, while repeatedly saying "I knew that answer. I knew that answer. She didn't call on me, I knew the answer". I'm getting teary eyed just writing this. That broke me y'all. Now I'm the one flipping the fuck out. My feelings are hurt for this child. As I watch the child cry, whole class sitting in silence, shocked because the student is not acting up. They are actually trying to make the student feel better. And here goes the teacher acting as if she doesn't notice! So, I cursed her ass out in front of the entire class. Now maybe it wasn't right to go about it this way, but I did not care. Because we talked about this after the last incident in detail beyond what I said at the door, and you intentionally did it again?! So I had to let this teacher know, "you got me fucked up. I am not the one. I don't care about CPS or this job, right is right and wrong is wrong. How dare you allow this child to hold their hand up for 2 minutes straight and not call on them!?!?! I'm sitting in the back and watching you purposely ignore this student." I say a few more choice words…and then tell the teacher "the shit BET NOT happen again!" Startled by me checking her in front of the class she comes over to the student trying to apologize and making up excuses as to why she didn't call on them. I told her "ain't nobody tryna hear that shit" and I tell my student "let's go."

(cause now I'm the one that needs to calm down haha). I felt bad because I don't like cursing in front of young children, but then I was like some of the students cuss more than me. I always want to lead by example and that was, not necessarily, an example I wanted to set for that age group, but then again it was. I was conflicted. I want my students, all students and especially Black students to stand up for what they believe in, and never let anyone mistreat them, or do anything to them that would harm their confidence. Nor make them think that they are not good enough, not worthy enough or don't know anything. Because life for most of us African Americans is a challenge straight out the womb. And we must overcome it. So yeah, I cursed that teacher smooth out. I knew they weren't going to fire me until the job was done. I was over the school anyway.

After leaving the class, I calm the crying child down. I tell that child how proud I was of them for not acting out even though I knew they were hurt. The child says to me "I knew the answer Ms. Johnson, I really knew the answer". I say, "remind me of the question again and tell me the answer." The student does and I say "awesome you are correct!" and then we celebrate. I tell the child to keep their head held high, even when teachers like that mistreat them. We talked about why I cursed the teacher out, and my feelings about the situation. I tell the student to not let that situation deter them from doing their best because the teacher is ignorant. The child then says to me, "She's really not my teacher, you are", and I say "you're right, but it's certain things in the near future that you will have no choice but to complete with her, because they won't let me stand in completely for you". (They wouldn't even let me come to the IEP meetings y'all. Even though the option was there, because I was the one doing all of the work, but the teacher didn't want me there and the administration allowed it). I openly expressed to the child how I felt about that teacher. Then I explained what was expected from me, from the teacher and from the child. Then we went back to class.

Now I know you all may be thinking that this is a long story for challenge. It has been my greatest challenge thus far. That whole situation was a challenge. Remind you, all of this was being done in the midst of me still having to restrain the child on certain days from hurting themselves, by banging their head on the wall, floor etc. It was not an easy task. I had to do everything with this child in LOVE, while challenging and being creative. Back em up, push em forward, while keeping them safe. Balance. Can you also say tired? These types of situations are what creates a deeper level of understanding and empathy for the parent. Nonetheless I got the child into a SPED class. By the time the child got to the special needs class within the 6-month time frame, the child knew all their ABC's, how to recognize both upper case and lower case letters. Knew 24 of the 26 letter sounds. How to spell their first and last name. Write (it was at a super slow pace but was getting better) They could count to 20 already, so we were able to get to counting to 100, and recognize numbers 1-12. Read basic sight words, and sight word books, walk in a line, raise hand, have conversations with peers without fighting, use the computer, feel confident in themselves and express themselves in a more controlled manner. We were also starting a little on basic math. I'm probably forgetting some things because it was a lot, but those were key! And I know some of you may be thinking this isn't a lot, Oh but it is! I was able to teach this child the basic foundations for what they needed to grow. Why was all of this possible? Because not only did I challenge myself to do more, I challenged that child and everyone else around that child as well. Then I got fired for my hard work, and they gave the other teacher credit for what I did. I was deemed "not being a team player". That would soon be the terminology I would constantly hear, no matter what type of school I worked for, whenever I decided to do what was right for either myself or a student or my class. But I don't care and I will continue to accept all challenges and hope that this story will encourage you to do so too.

This story has led me to my last and final C for bonding. Which is to correct. I'm not sure if you noticed in the story how much correction I had to do with the child, and even with the teacher. Even though with the teacher it may not have been the most respectful or professional way. Ehh, I was young, in my early twenties, and if someone kept mistreating your child, wouldn't you curse them out too?

A lot of times we have to first see what's wrong and then correct the child, and sometimes even correct ourselves. When I redirect children, sometimes I have to correct the way I may challenge the child to move forward. Whether it's me stepping back and looking at the situation to notice what's going on. Slowing the pace up, and adding an encouraging word or two, or knowing when to push and when not to push. See, when the child acted a plum fool in the challenge story, even though I did not stop the child in the moment, I still corrected them afterwards. In my mind it was a double correction, ha! One for the child and one for the teacher, even though the actual correction for the teacher didn't come until after I cursed her ass out. I guess she was embarrassed because it certainly didn't happen again. But in my opinion that teacher needed correction and nothing else was getting through to her. She didn't realize how her actions were affecting the student.

If you sit back and observe, you will see the mistakes and the growth. It will even show you the mistakes being made and the growth on your end. Observation will always let you know how to respond. Correction comes after the observation, (something we will talk about a little more later on). I will always encourage you to let your child try first, before correcting them and showing them the correct way to do something. It will save you both a headache.

Because for the most part, a child would know when they are doing something wrong, or not being the best or doing the best in a situation. Instead of saying "didn't I tell you", try saying, "you got it, you just need to work on this." Then take the time to show them over and over again until they get it. That correction, then becomes a practice. Flowing right on into the letter D for dum dum dum dummm…discipline and development.

Chapter D

D *is for*
Discipline & Development

Discipline is such a touchy subject for people. But honestly, I simply don't think people actually know what it means to discipline. So let's do some vocabulary shall we. Let's take it back old school, go get your Webster's dictionary. Look at ALL the definitions. Now let's look at the one that says to train or develop by instruction and exercise specifically in self-control. Now let me ask you this, do you think enough of us are doing that? No. I believe we like to focus on and use the definition that says to punish or penalize for the sake of enforcing obedience and perfecting moral character. I think the problem with this one though is that last part of the sentence, which is perfecting moral character. Hmmmm. In my humble opinion, a lot of people's morals are in no way shape or form perfect for the most part. And with that thought process, are we now enforcing immoral behavior? Beyond that, does the Webster second definition for discipline now become the first definition? It says discipline is control gained by enforcing obedience or order? Now read all of that again. Let's chat.My personal belief is that you have to balance all of those definitions. Typically, we don't. We usually do one or the other, and then depending on your ethnic background you may not discipline at all. With me being a teacher, over time I have come to see how corporal punishment can be beneficial and detrimental. In school back in the day, they chose to discipline you by making you write lines, balancing books in the corner, and sometimes running stairs. Then other schools gave you that "board of education". You were then on line. (If some of you are wondering what on line mean, go ask a member of the Divine 9). Because of the children who were "on line", they took discipline out of most schools. One minute holding children accountable was ok, but adults took it too far, and they took it completely away in most states. That could possibly be by design too, because our children were better behaved then, in my opinion. But now there is no accountability for the children, and none for the administration either. There is no sense of balance, and I believe we have to balance it all. With changes happening over time within the school system, I feel like that is what has helped me. Because discipline has been a technique I use to build better relationships with my students. We have to balance these definitions, but we don't. What do I mean by that? Well it's simple actually. It is a must that we train or develop by instruction. How do we expect children to learn? At the same time, we must understand children are going to be children. They are inquisitive beings. They learn by doing, seeing, touching, tasting, smelling, and feeling. In other words, "they gone try you!" Just be prepared for it. Expect it. And when they do, guess what, you have to be disciplined too, because monkey see monkey do. Children learn first from what you do, and then, waaaayyyyy later on from what you say.

So often we try to force our children and students to do right, when we ourselves aren't doing right. But we want to hand out ass whoopings and curse them out, causing all this social and emotional damage that then gets passed down from generation to generation, calling it discipline. Do I think there's a better way to go about it? Yes. In my humble belief it's simple. Be the example that you wish to see first. Don't be so quick to spank. Learn to give adequate instructions. Teach them the things you think they should know. Once you do, now it's time to hold them accountable for their actions and choices. If they continue to act up, ask yourself why first? It can be an underlying reason that would require more than an ass whooping. Teach restraint and patience. If you have to tap a hand, make sure you are repeating why what they're doing isn't right. Take something away that they love, or love to do as a consequence, with an explanation as to why. Always have a conversation about whatever they did wrong, and why it is wrong! I mean, as I say all this, notice how we always come back to the rule of instruction. Example. "How do we exercise self control?" "Do we get upset every time we don't get our way?" "No." But if they do, ignore them…that's a form of discipline. "We not happy with the amount of chips we got…ok, really?" Take em all back, now they don't have anything. Form of discipline. "We hitting?" "How would you like it if someone hit you?" "Do you want me to show you how it feels?" Questions and conversation, a form of discipline. "Are you screaming at the top of your lungs?" "Ok, that's fine, go over there to the room and scream all you want. When you're done let me know, and close the door cause don't nobody want to hear all that." A form of discipline. All needing to come back to a conversation at the end after everyone is calm.

See at school, especially in early childhood education we aren't allowed to hit the children at all. We would go to jail, or lose our job and everything we've worked hard for. So good teachers, we have to get creative in the ways we choose to discipline. Trust and believe, I have done it mostly through conversation and taking something away. I don't even think that we are allowed to take away honestly, but I do it so much, who cares. I'm the adult in a classroom of 12 toddlers who are one…or twenty 3 year old's or 45 kindergartners…trust and believe something is being taken away. I have to control the class and keep them safe the best way I can. "Oh, do you think I'm giving parties to a misbehaving class?" No ma'am, no sir. "You think we're going to paint and do a big messy project that can be a lot of fun with a class that's uncontrollable?" No ma'am no sir. "Oh, you don't know how to walk in the hall during recess time?" Ok let me lecture you on what we not gone do, for about 45 minutes. Discipline. Oh you're hitting that child and the child finally hits you back, I see it and I turn the other cheek… a form of discipline. You bite, and a child finally bites you back. Discipline. Sometimes I don't even have to step in for discipline to happen. Sometimes the lessons come through peers, but what we will do is talk about why it happened.

We have to remember that discipline is a balance between training, developing, exercising self-control, penalizing wrong behavior to strengthen morals, while also enforcing obedience to gain order and control, in which I would say, for reasons of safety. We have to balance all of this, or else we are not disciplining. We may just be harming our children, physically, mentally and emotionally for no reason. The lack of discipline can be just as dangerous and hurtful as well. Not having boundaries with your children should never be an option. Letting them do whatever, whenever, all the time is not good. It shows a lack of self-control, that could end up getting them hurt unknowingly in the future.

In early childhood education, we are taught to be proactive more so than reactive in everything that we do. We have to monitor, observe, and forecast or foresee every possible situation in the classroom that can possibly happen before it happens. We also have to train and prepare for it. Especially emergency situations. If you are reactive to everything, there are more chances of everything going wrong, in an unfortunate chain of events. What does this have to do with discipline you ask? Well in the beginning I said we have a hard time discipling our children, because we ourselves aren't disciplined. Be proactive in everything you do. Train yourself for those moments that your children try you, so that you will be prepared to discipline them in a more appropriate manner. Not just ass whoopings, yelling, or in some cases, nothing at all. If you understand that children are going to be children, and this is what they do, you will be more prepared mentally. I encourage everyone to understand that while disciplining, and to make sure your discipline practices have a healthy balance. All in all, sometimes what you think is discipline, is really not. I got whoopins up until the 5th grade, then my dad started lecturing me. I don't know why he stopped whopping me. Maybe he realized it wasn't effective. I kept getting whooped for the same thing over and over. The last time I got a whooping, it was me and my sister receiving ones. She cried, I didn't and then I got up and teased her for crying. I laugh as I type this cause evidently that whoopin didn't phase me. I was like, "this is what I do, I get whooped for everything Ha!" I swear that was the last day, and man when I started receiving lectures, I literally asked my Dad if he could just whoop me instead. Hahaha. He said no and I started crying! Ha! I did not want to hear that shit! Do you hear me! Every moment after me having stopped getting whoopins was torture! The having to do everything over, expressing myself, opening up, explaining myself, reiterating back what was said to me. I was like "please whoop me!" Whoopins were easier. It hurt for the moment, I would be mad for a second, and then I went on "bout my business." But not with those damn lectures. It felt like it lasted a lifetime, and the majority of those lessons did.

At the end of the day when we discipline our children, the end goal should be communicating the message or lesson you want them to receive. If the goal of disciplining is to train, instruct, develop and strengthen, you have to ask yourself if you are doing that. Ask yourself how you are doing that, and most importantly do you see the results? If not, I would say you're not disciplining.

Moving right into Development. It's this terminology being used often called age appropriate development. It is often used in childcare, and I absolutely hate it. To be honest I think it's a whole hunk of bullshit that administration in affluent school types use just so they can justify reasons as to why you should stick to their sorry curriculum and rules. (I have a thing about curriculums, I don't necessarily care for them, but understand their usefulness. I also feel you should be prepared to come up with your own any day of the week, and I should not be forced to stick to something that isn't working for me, and most importantly the children). But that's another story for another book. I mean think about it, it's a big contradiction to say children are like sponges between the ages of birth to 5. To say it is the most critical years of a child's life, the foundation of which they learn best, which I wholeheartedly believe. Then turnaround and fix your lips to tell me what I am doing in my classroom with my students, who are learning expeditiously!? Who are having fun!? Growing!? And want to continue to learn!?!?! Is not age and developmentally appropriate?!?!? Not only that, you haven't even spent 5 minutes with the child? How would you know?!? How are you going to tell me, the teacher, who is spending 8 to 12 hours of my life with this student on an everyday basis, what is not developmentally appropriate for them? No ma'am, no sir! Have several seats.

My philosophy is this. No two children are the same. Their backgrounds may be similar, but not the same. The way they learn and understand things might be similar, but are not the same. And their interest and the way they learn may be similar, but it is not the same! So yes Billie is only able to count to 10, but Willie can count to 100. Because Willie can count to 100, I encourage him to move on to the next steps so he won't get bored, which is number recognition. I want him to start recognizing numbers 1-50. You gone tell me not to do that, because it's not in the curriculum, because it isn't developmentally appropriate for his age?! According to who!??! You?! Because it certainly isn't the child!

Due to the admin or that teacher thinking that way, they have a school full of behavior problems, instead of children learning. Simply because you want the Willies to wait on the Billies. When the Billies can be encouraged by the Willies, if you don't shame them or force them to move or grow faster. Then it becomes you are pouring into one, more than the other. That for me is simply not right! And it goes back to my challenge word. In my humble opinion, we are not developmentally challenging our children enough. Since we are on a definition kick with these D words, let's look into the definition of development in early childhood education. Child development focuses on the development in the areas of cognitive, social and emotional, language, speech, and physical (fine and gross motor). It sets the foundation for life long learning (or what I call, the willingness to learn), and mental and physical help. (Key word foundation). Now let's look up the regular definition of development. There are several, but my favorites are, "to set forth or make clear by degrees or detail. Expound. To work out the possibilities of. To make active or promote the growth of." And last but not least, "to cause to evolve or unfold gradually: to lead or conduct something through a succession of the states or changes each of which is preparatory for the next." If that last definition ain't key!! (That's slang for those of you who don't know, the last definition is spot on) Let's sit in "the preparatory for the next." In my line of work. That's all I am doing!! I am preparing my students for the next teacher, next level, next grade, next milestone, the next something! And just in case they get a very sucky teacher, I want them to be above and beyond what the grade level expects of them, if THEY are showing ME they are READY. Furthermore, it is my job to set forth or make clear the details they learn. I am to promote their growth and development. In hopes that they evolve mentally, physically, spiritually, emotionally, intellectually, cognitively and so on and so forth. Better than me or any adult they know or come across. Be BETTER THAN ME. I also feel I should not be doing this alone! But in conjunction with their parents! Because why? You are your child's first and most important teacher. Of course all of this is based upon what that child is ready for, and NOT WHAT I WANT THEM TO BE READY FOR. It's not about me, it's about them. Because a lot of parent's do that too! "Oh he's not ready to use the potty, I don't think he's ready for potty training". No ma'am, sir, it's you. You're not ready. You are being lazy. Your whole child is taking his diaper off and slinging poop everywhere, oh he's ready. You just don't want to clean up the accidents. Change the sheets when they pee in the middle of the night, wake 'em up during a nap to make them go potty, throw the poopy draws away and get more. It is YOU. Not them. If your child can come and verbally tell me they pooped their pants!!! They are ready! But I can't and won't waste my time sitting them on the pot, when you are not doing it at home, because my hard work will go down the drain every weekend, and I will constantly be starting over. Why would a child sit on the pot, if he knows all he has to do is poop and lay down and you will come and change him. I'll keep pooping on myself too if I know I can get away with doing it. We have to look at the signs and be willing and ready to put in the work for the development of our children. Us putting in that work is what creates that bond. We should be aware of developmentally appropriate practices and use them to challenge their growth. (Just so you know age-appropriate development and developmentally- appropriate practices are not the same and aren't used the same in childcare. Again, I think someone made it up) We should not want to hold our children or students back in any way, shape, form, or fashion in the areas of cognitive, social and emotional, physical, mental, language, and speech development. (Imma throw mathematics in there too just because.) Don't ever think they are too young for advancement, without spending the proper time with them or trying to teach them something new. Teach them while they are young the correct things. Remember the quote, "it is easier to raise strong children than to repair broken men." (Fredrick Douglas, one of my favorite quotes) It's true, and how we choose to develop our children and their mindset from a young age means everything. Telling a teacher or a parent that something isn't developmentally age appropriate when you haven't met, talked to, observed, or spent any time with the student, is like telling them they are not worthy of knowledge. Don't ever let a person tell you what your child is not capable of doing! Especially when you know without a shadow of a doubt, they are.

Chapter E

E *is for*
Engage, Embarrass, Educate, Energy & Emotional Development

Let's start with Engage, shall we. It's quite simple honestly. I don't know what else to say except engage with your child or student. I mean, I want you to insert yourself into everything your child does. Well not everything, give them their space sometimes, but be there. If your child talks to you about something, especially if it's exciting to them, PLEASE FOR THE LOVE OF GOD, TALK BACK! JEEZE. I can't stand to see children talking to adults, and no one is talking back. Do you know how belittling that is? You just ignore them until they start screaming and hollering. It's crazy. Talk to them. You'll be surprised to see what happens when you talk back.

While you're engaging with your child, don't be afraid to embarrass yourself. Not the child. Don't ever embarrass the child if you can help it. But embarrass yourself. Don't be afraid to act silly, sing a song, do a dance while you're being active and engaging with your child. Don't you love to hear your child laugh? It's the sweetest thing. Plus it's good for the soul. So go ahead, don't be afraid to make a fool of yourself in the name of love, for your child. Although, as they get older, they may deem this as less funny. Haha.

Educate in everything that you do. You know that word 'why' your child eventually throws at you all the time? Don't run from it, and please don't say, "because I said so". (rolls eyes). Give the actual reason so that they can learn and understand. Explain in detail if you can. This opens up their level of understanding and is great for comprehension reasons. Eventually they will stop asking you why so much and start telling you why, and how and when and where. Ha Ha.

While you are doing all this, the embarrassing, the engaging, the educating with your child, don't forget to exude positive energy. Your energy says everything! Children can feel it, and they can sense it. They know when you are happy, angry, sad, annoyed, hurt, tired and the list goes on and on. They can feel it all. That's why when children tell me their teacher is mean, one too many times I'm looking into it and observing it. I have actually worked with children who just weren't vibin with certain teachers, and a lot of the times they were right. That teacher's energy was off towards them. It may not be towards all of the children in the room, but you can definitely tell when the teacher had something against a few select students. With that being said, you know what time it is.

Example time, which means story time. In 2010, I worked at this center in Illinois. This center was mixed, it had a lot of Black and Hispanic children. Well in my class I had a child whose parent was recovering from meth and a whole lotta other issues. In the class right next to me, they had this child's sibling. Now my class was a 3 year old class, and of course because I'm the teacher, we were rockin' and rollin' in there. Me and my Co-teacher (R.I.P) we had the routines and everything down packed. We worked in our strengths and not in our weaknesses. Anyway, the next class over was the Pre-k/Kindergarten room, in which I was preparing my children for. My student sibling, who was in that class, was delayed. That child didn't speak much and had some learning disabilities. Both students were suffering from issues at home. My student had anger issues, would throw chairs, cuss you out, throw food and so on, but was very, very smart. We worked on that child's anger issues. I didn't know anything other than their sibling had a big learning disability and wouldn't talk to anyone when starting. Now at this school, they were the minority, because they were white. Just like the students, the majority of the teachers at the school were Black or Hispanic as well. This child's class had two teachers too, one Black and one White.

Now I don't know what was happening this one particular month, but the teachers next door were always yelling at my student sibling. Well, they yelled all the time, but it was starting to get ridiculous. Then I would hear stuff like, "I can't take this, you stink". "Go to the bathroom". "I'm not bout to be cleaning you up every day", "Uuughhhh", "This child is getting on my nerves", and then you would hear a loud humming sound coming from the child. Then I would hear "Be quiet" "Shut up", "You gone wake the class", "Get over here", and then the humming sound would get louder. Now I'm like, is it some illegal stuff going on in this class? So I poke my head in and say "Hey everything ok? I can hear y'all all the way over in my class. What's the problem?" Then they would be like "Ms. Johnson get this child cause Imma bout to lose it!" I'm like "what's the problem?" They say, "the child won't go to sleep, then they like to hum and make a lot of noise and then to make it worse, the child would sit there and pee on themselves." Well in childcare, when teachers say imma bout to lose it if you don't get this child, that's a sign for a mental breakdown. (Yes we be bout ready to lose our shits sometimes too) So of course I'm like "give me the child's cot, and from now on, anytime you don't want to deal with the child just send the child to me." Now y'all know that child was in my class damn near all day for about a month right?

Anyways the child did stink. But the child smelled that way from the time they arrived at school. That child's sibling did too. So what we did in my class was wash their clothes, and all the extra clothes that were brought from home as well, and kept it in their cubbie. So we started to do that for their sibling too. Now y'all know how I feel about communication. So every morning, no matter how the child smelled, when that child came into my class I gave that child a hug. Asked that child how they were doing, and changed their clothes out if we had extra. We had routines in my class, so that child had to fall in line with that routine, and did so effortlessly. When it was time for a nap, the child did hum. I would go over there and say "hey it's ok to hum, but can you hum a little quietly, we don't want to wake your friends". Guess what y'all. The child stopped humming, and while I sat next to them, went to sleep. Now, the child did have accidents, and when the child did, I did not yell, or get upset or anything. I would say "it's ok, we gotta change your clothes. Let's go to the bathroom." While in the bathroom changing that child's clothes, I would explain why it's important to use the bathroom. Then told that child, they were smart, they can do it, and that we are going to practice. I would ask if they understood, and the child would nod yes. After changing that child, the child would give me a hug.

So for about two weeks that's what we did, potty train. The child would go to the pot with the other students in the class. During naps I would wake the child up and make them go potty and then help them get back to sleep. After waking up from their nap, we would celebrate. I would give a big hug and say how proud I was. I would then say, "go potty." And the child went and pottied. The child wouldn't smell like pee so much coming to school anymore. The child was also happier, and started trying to talk more. Of course when that child's original teacher started noticing, she was like "what you do?" I simply said, "talk to em, and gave lots of hugs, and washed their clothes". I'm like "you do know what they are going through at home right?" The teacher was like "yea," and I'm like, "well this is their safe haven. We can't be mean. Trust your student's sibling be trying me too, but it's a better way. They not gone do what you want them to do by yelling and being negative to them. They probably see or experience that enough at home. Also mom just got them back, she's trying, we gotta help. We shouldn't do anything to set them back." Annnnnnnd of course after that, after allllllllll the work I put into the child, the Director comes and says that the child has to go back to their class because of the age dynamic and yadayada yada right. So, I'm like "ok." "Whatever." The child goes back, the child starts having issues in that class again, and all my hard work was slowing going down the drain. I had to start going into their class during nap time to check on the child, put the child to sleep and encourage the child to participate in class. The child did, while I was there. But other than that, gave the teachers a hard time. They would come and tell me that the child wasn't cooperating and wouldn't go to the pot, but wasn't peeing on themselves too often. So I would stick my head in the class and have the child come potty with my class whenever we pottied. It worked. The child wanted to see me and just know that I was there most of the time, and that I still cared. So I made it a point to show that to the child everyday. I share this story to show the difference in energy. As dynamic and energized as my energy can be, it also exudes a caring me as well. I genuinely want to help children, no matter what their background is, because we are all going through something. I would hope that if I had children, the teachers or adults around them wouldn't mistreat my child no matter the circumstance of our race, background, abilities and so on. Make sure your energy is great. It matters. It can be the difference in your child or student giving you a hard time or working with you.

Make sure your energy is on point, and if it's not, guess what? Share that! It is totally ok to express to your children that you are not having a great day, or you are not feeling your best. Educate them on the way you are feeling and even express to them why you are feeling that way. I mean when you do this, it does wonders! Don't believe me? Try it! Do you know how many times students have felt my energy and have made me feel better?! It is almost impossible to stay mad or sad working with children for long.

Whether I express it or not, they always find a way to make me laugh. Then it's like the more I share with them, the more they get me! Ha! Man, it's crazy and kinda cool! Like for instance, one time in class I was not happy because the assistant director was on some BS early in the morning. Trying to place blame on me for something dealing with the computer, after I kept telling her ass, I didn't know what the hell she was talking about because I never used her computer. It irked me so, because nobody wants to hear all that first thing in the morning as soon as they get in, especially when I don't know what the hell you are talking about. So, it got on my nerves. I was sitting in the dramatic play area, clearly with an attitude trying to calm down, when one of my students was like "Ms. J what's wrong?" Then another student comes up after him and says, "She's annoyed". Now I couldn't help but to burst out laughing out loud, because not only was he correct, but I was also proud. Now why was I proud you ask. Because annoyed was a vocabulary word we had went over, a month before. In my efforts to help them understand what annoyed meant, or looked like, I used to always make a face. They had to make their annoyed face as well. Well, it was written all over my face, I didn't have to say a word! (If you didn't sing that part, something is totally wrong with you). I guess he read my expression and called it like he saw it, and was completely right. In a matter of seconds, I was no longer annoyed, and I explained to them what made me annoyed in the first place, and we had a whole conversation about it. It was awesome.

The knowledge and understanding of how I felt just by looking at me, cheered me up so much, because it showed me that me and my students, were dope. We had built relationships, and not only that, they were listening to my teachings in class. I could be having the worst day and the children could change my energy, and vice versa. Even in moments where I am tired or not feeling well. When I talk to them about it, and they can visually see it and feel that this is not normal Ms. J, I ask them to help me out by using their indoor voices, listening ears, and settle disputes without me. They be on it too. They become the best helpers at this moment and they also smother me with love as well. Giving lots of hugs, and asking lots of questions about me feeling better. It's wonderful. So always be mindful of your energy, and communicate the type of energy you want to get across, even when you may not be able to give it at that moment.

Next you also want to be mindful of your student's energy! Their energy controls the pace of the lessons. Sometimes, they just may not be feeling it, and that's ok. Be mindful of it, and don't make your lessons too long. That might be a day where they are playing more, and doing one on ones more than group work at the carpet. Why make your day harder than it has to be because your students' energy is off. Observation is key in this. Because they may be having a real chill day, or they may be having one of those days where they're energy is off the mutha fuckin chain!!! Oh' and usually on those days, any and everything that can go wrong usually does. Ha ha ha!! But don't fret! Take a chill pill! Yes YOU! The chill pill isn't going to work on these types of days for the children, but outside will! This is the time you do as much music and movement, or outside play as possible. Let them be free! Remember, their energy controls the pace of the lessons. No need to drive yourself crazy. Typically when my class is super energetic, to the point it's causing disruptions, fights, arguments and I'm on the verge of a meltdown cause I just can't that day. ALL of my lessons turn into outside lessons! Lol that's my secret. We talking about animals, we going on a nature walk, bear hunt, something. Then imma let them play outside. I'm also going to make sure I play with them! This ensures that they are running around, hopping, jumping, skipping, but mostly chasing me. I get my exercise in for the day, and they get tired. Win win. What am I doing? Burning that energy! If we are stuck inside the class, because it's a rainy day, it's music and movement time. We are singing, playing follow the leader, playing listen and move activities, and more. I grab those musical instruments, and we become a marching band. The classroom becomes noisy, yes, but not because they are fighting and yelling at one another. Not because they are chasing each other around and hurting themselves. And not because they are crying every 15 seconds over a toy. The class room activities are still structured even though it is loud. What am I doing? While burning their energy, I am controlling the movement and type of energy that is flowing inside the class. I call it organized chaos, because although it is loud, we are still able to have organized fun, and they are not tearing up the class and acting a fool. Doing this tires them out and calms them down. I know a lot of teachers hate letting their students play with the musical instruments, (which never made sense to me), but they are there for a reason. I don't know how you would rather let them be all over the place, stressing you out, when you could get up and control the pace of the class. Stop being lazy, and lame. That's why your students give you a hard time. You don't know how to read the room and control the energy that flows through there. The student's energy matters, just as much as yours. You can't be afraid to have fun with your students. If you are worried about losing control of the classroom, what you do is redirect the attention and focus back on you. You do this by recouping. It's like pressing that start over button. You pivot, to readjust what is going on in class. Bring them back to the carpet, have a small talk about the rules and what you want to see versus what you don't. Then start the fun all over again. That's how you keep control of the situation. I don't care how many times you gotta do it. On an energetic day, that is how you keep control of the situation. Your energy stays fun and calm, yet stern, while you allow the children the freedom to hop, jump, skip, sing and play around the class to burn that energy. Make sure when you are considering the flow and tone of the class for the day, you take in consideration all that is involved. You are not in the classroom by yourself. Nor are you teaching yourself. Your students' energy matters. Just like you would want them to be mindful of your energy or feelings on a not so good day for yourself, you have to be mindful of their not so good days. It requires balance. Our not so good days for students are days when we lack energy. In return, their energetic days are usually the not so good days for us. Especially if we are not equipped to handle their energy. In which I say, every teacher should be equipped to handle children's energy.

Last but not least on this E list is emotional development. In fact, imma let emotional development lead us into our next set of words in the alphabet, because all of it would tie into emotional development. Emotional development is the journey of processing our feelings.

Chapter F

F *is for*
Feelings, Focus & Fun

Let's connect this word of emotional development to this word feeling. What is that? Simple, how do you feel? Then allow yourself to sit in that emotion, and process it out. For my culture, I feel this is a big problem. We have a hard time processing our emotions. We either don't sit in them at all, or we sit in them too long. I barely see balance here. For the most part, we are holding these feelings in, and we never seem to let those feelings out. Why, because we don't often hear "it's ok, let it out." We tend to hear, "shut up and be strong." We are made to feel weak if we feel anything other than strong. Then we push that onto our children. Crazy right?! I too have suffered from this, and it still affects me a little till this day.

We say things like, "stop crying before I give you something to cry about." As if what the children are already crying about isn't validated. We are really hard on our little boys. We tell them, "men don't cry," "chest out, chin up, keep it in." Well sorry to tell you sir, madam. Your 1 year old son isn't a man, he's a little boy, and they do cry. What emotional development is designed to do is help children to identify their emotions, and address it without shaming the child. We have an array of feelings, sad, mad, happy, proud, nervous, calm, annoyed and the list goes on and on. I encourage you to talk about the definitions of these words and feelings with your children. Then whenever they come up, address them.

For instance, toddlers are nonverbal for the most part, especially if you are not speaking to your child in complete sentences. Let's say your child is the only child, and they get introduced to a social setting with other children for the first time ever. Sharing is a big issue, why? Because they don't typically have to share at home, it's just them. So when Ty comes over into their space, and starts playing with something they may not even be playing with, it's an issue. Why? Because according to that child, everything in that space is considered what? "MINES." It's theirs and you are not to touch it. They don't understand that they are in a public space, or around other children. All they understand is what they are used to, and that is playing by themselves. Therefore, when Ty comes over and takes a toy, all hell breaks loose and your child loses it. Their feelings may very well be hurt, they may very well be confused or angry. Because why? They don't have these issues at home, and for the life of them they can't understand why you decide to reprimand them now. They are feeling all these ways, and start to hit, fall out and have tantrums. Now, what should be happening is you explaining to them why they have to share. But you aren't. You say things like "stop all that, before I spank you", or worse you say to yourself or others around you things like, "this child is bad, ugghh gets on my nerves, spoiled butt!" No one is talking to the child. No one is explaining to the child, it's ok to be upset, it's not ok to act a fool. That they understand they want all the toys, but they can't have them because it is not theirs, and they are not at home. Now because of that, this child is falling out and acting a plum fool the entire time. They are upset. Let them be upset. Acknowledge that they are upset. Tell them that you understand why they are upset, yet correct the problem. And guess what, it WILL take some time to get through to them what is and isn't right, and why. But YOU have to stay consistent. Remember once they are calm, those are the best times to have conversations. Speaking in complete sentences, saying things like "I know you are used to playing by yourself at home. But we are not at home, and all of these toys do not belong to you. Therefore, you can't get upset when someone wants to come play. It's nice to play with other children, you should try it. It may make you happy. Sharing isn't all bad. There is a time to share and a time not to. This is the time to share." A simple conversation like that can go a long way. Reiterating "We don't kick, bite or scream when we don't get our way", explains to them that this isn't the right way to handle their emotions when something doesn't go their way. You should then describe the behavior you wish to see from them, instead of constantly pointing out what they did wrong.

When we acknowledge the behavior and feelings, it says I see you, and sometimes, I understand. After we have acknowledged the behavior, if they are still acting up, walk away. It says, "I'll give you some space to calm down." When they are calm and ready to listen and or talk, speaking to them about the situation says "I care." It can also say, "I'm not mad", depending on the conversation. In the calm state, we should be helping them to identify why they are upset, and some things we can do to get them back to their happy space. (Which should be super easy for most children, because they typically don't stay mad long). Talking this out helps them to process and identify what happened to make them upset, and why or how to overcome it. Letting them know what is and isn't right, says "I will hold you accountable for your actions." Not addressing this properly from the start is what leads to behavior problems. Processing feelings and helping them to recognize or think their way through situations is very important. Too many children lack this skill. These effects last all the way up into adult age. (Then we wonder why we can't properly communicate and express feelings to each other as adults…it starts here people!) This in contrast with discipline is something that we don't do enough of. It's time to change that.

Focus. As we know children's attention spans are short. They are easily distracted. As quickly as you can snap your fingers, their attention has moved on to something else. So how do we get them to focus and pay attention? Well my biggest and most successful way is by making things fun! Through redirection, (something we will get more into later on in the book), and attention grabbers. Right now until this day, I can go into any classroom, and just start singing and grab the attention of the children. Once this happens, their focus is right on me, and once I have it, I have to act quickly.

Attention grabbers really work hand in hand with embarrassment. Remember we can't be afraid to embarrass ourselves. If someone came on the train dressed like cookie monster trying to sell cookies, and you have never seen that before, it'll get your attention right? That's an attention grabber, something out of the blue that will grab your child's attention, and have them focused on you. Some of these attention grabbers can make you look or feel silly, like a grown man in a cookie monster costume riding the train.

Now how do we get them to focus on their work? Through repetition and breaks. Helping them focus works in conjunction with challenging them in meaningful and creative ways as we discussed earlier in the book. Knowing when to push and when to stop is key. Taking away distractions is also key. Music, TV, toys, anything distracting. In a classroom it may be children playing loudly with each other, and calling friends names. I know you're like, well in a classroom, how would you keep those distractions down. In older classrooms 3 and up, usually by rotating centers. But if we have to test the children and I know that the child is easily distracted, I will pull them into another classroom with no students or wait until all children are sleep during naptime. Sometimes one on ones help children focus better as well, as we learned in the challenge story in chapter C. Once you work with the child, you can slowly work them into group settings with more distractions. This helps them build their focus as well. With toddlers, it's a waiting game. Because as soon as they do the thing that they are focused on, they are moving right on to the next. So the trick is to keep them there for as long as possible, waiting their turn. What do I mean by that, well it's time for another story.

I was working as a toddler teacher at a school in Tennessee. I had this wonderful child in my class who was off the chain! I loved this child, this child gave me a run for my money every day, nonetheless, that was my baby. Now toddlers want to do everything! And when I say toddlers, I mean children between the ages of 1 and 2 just so y'all know. (I know medically or professionally the word toddler is used until age 3 but not for me, I also hate counting by months, but understand why we have to do it sometimes. But don't tell me your child is 48 months when I ask you how old they are, if you don't just say 4, ughh). Anyways, toddlers be everywhere, and you have to have your routine down packed to get them to the point where they know what to do without you having to say anything. This goes for every child and age group, but it is especially important with toddlers. Consistency is a must! (Remember that when you are looking for a childcare center for your baby). Now this child, like I said, off the chain. Hitting, biting, smack in, and so on. You could not leave this child by themselves for too long, or something was about to go down haha. So this child was my pocket buddy a lot! Because I spent time getting to know my students, I knew what everyone loved, and this child particularly shared a love for art just like me. I used art everyday to teach everything in that class. But one day by accident, I noticed that I had made this child wait too long and they ended up being last. But the child sat in that chair at that table with their hands in their lap until it was their turn. I was like wow, although it wasn't my intention to make the child last, it helped me be in better control of the class. How? Because the child that caused the most problems when they were not around me, was sitting next to me the whole time patiently waiting. So, you know what I started to do right? That's right, make that child wait.

This was new to me, because before then I had always worked with the older students 3-5 because that's what I preferred. At other centers when I was in toddler classrooms, they just let them do whatever. There weren't any routines, and they wouldn't allow me to put routines into place. I did not stay very long with those centers. I don't like unorganized chaos. It doesn't sit right with my spirit. So accidentally, I learned a new trick, and it worked no matter what class I went to. When the child is super interested in something and really wants to do it, you have their attention a little longer, until it's done. Once it's done, they turn back into the little Tasmanian devils they are.

Focusing is a time management thing as well. When children lack focus, and even adults, it takes up unnecessary time. When you are unable to redirect that focus back to the lesson at hand, and quickly, you have now wasted time. That's time that could be going towards something else. A great way to help children refocus so that neither of your time is wasted, (if you the adult is patient enough) is to let them know that if they don't focus and pull through whatever the lesson may be, their time into something else will be lessened. "Ok you have 1 hour of tablet time, but because you are not focusing, every minute that we waste getting this done will be taken away from your tablet time." Now if there is no way to get away from distractions, or you want to train them not to be easily distracted, I would use that strategy. Always remember children only come to an understanding of focusing through repetition and reiteration. So be patient. It's a slow process, and eventually they do get better. But that solely depends on the person who is working with them to help them get through. Focus is a form of discipline for both you and the child. Let's not act like there aren't adults who lose focus or patience faster than the children. Ha Ha. Ready to give up because something did not go their way the first time. Your child or student focus can be a direct reflection of yours, or lack thereof.

Now, for the last F word. My favorite, FUN. Ask yourself, who likes a boring teacher? Did y'all figure out a boring teacher you learned from? I'm still waiting from when I asked the question in

Chapter C with creativity. Let me guess. All that you can remember from that teacher or that class, was how you could not stand that teacher or that class! What was the point right? You can't think of one thing that you learned can you? Except maybe how to ditch that class. Let me tell you a secret. Making learning fun is like tricking your child or student into learning, without them even realizing what is going on. It's like when you put on some dance or transitional music from youtube and the children are laughing, dancing and singing along. Exercising without even realizing it. But then when you say, without music, and without a fun tone, give me 50 jumping jacks, they are tired at 10!! Ha ha! The minute you turn on that song, they give you 50 jumping jacks no problem.

Now I know many of you think that you are fun. Sorry to tell you this, but you are not! If your child or class huffs and puffs anytime you introduce a lesson, not for disciplinary reasons, you my friend are not fun. If your child or class tells you they are "boring" one to many times, they mean to say you are boring! (It's so funny, I come back to school after being absent and talk to my students. I say did you have fun. I was boring Ms. Johnson. We didn't do nothing. I be like, you were bored? They be like yeah we were so boring haha). Ummmmm you my friend are not fun, and may not even be teaching anything. If the child is telling you they are bored, that's a serious problem!

We talked about this in chapter C. You have to get creative when teaching! Even if the creative activity only gets you (the teacher) excited at first. Trust if you are truly excited, that momentum will rub off on them. Just think about it for a second. Even the activities that you may have hated, because they were torturous to you, but that parent or teacher was having the time of their life while teaching it to you, you remember it don't you? You remember their laugh and the stupid little faces they would make while you were doing the activity. None of it was funny to you, but somehow you remember. I know I can. All I am saying is, the lesson will be more memorable if someone is having fun. Boring teachers give off this aura like they hate their job and don't want to be there. And if you don't want to be there, what makes you think the children are going to want to be there? Have some energy! Get excited! Be involved! And most importantly have fun! Trust me, children will receive that and have fun learning too.

Chapter G

G *is for*
Guide

    G is for guide. As teachers and parents, it is our job to guide our children, don't you agree? The hard part comes when you are unable to guide without doing. What do I mean by this? To guide is to show through examples or direction. A lot of people mistake this for doing it for them. And that's where we mess up. You can't do it for them. How are they going to learn? Most importantly, what happens when you are no longer there? This is why we have 30 year old men and women still at home with their mamas, not knowing how to take care of themselves, and worse, not willing to learn. No guidance. Everything is being done for them. How do we get to that state with our children or classes? Well, by feeding them all the time and not allowing them to practice feeding themselves. All because we don't want to clean up the mess. By picking up their blocks and putting it away for them because it will take too long to teach them how to pick up after themselves…"I have better things to do." By picking out their clothes because, "my baby ain't gonna be looking crazy." Instead of teaching them how to shop and dress and letting them discover themselves. By filling out the paperwork for them to get into college instead of allowing them to do it on their own, or showing them how to do it in the first place. By doing their homework for them because you are too impatient to work with them. The list could go on and on. And before anyone gets upset and gets their panties in a bunch remember the B word balance. Understand there are levels to this. You have to balance the level of control you give them for various reasons of protection, safety, money, etc. I get that, but it's when you don't give the opportunity at all, that trouble will arise. The problem is you start to make the children a little messed up version of yourself, rather than letting them become who they are supposed to be. You start living the life you didn't have or you wanted to have through your children. Then when they get older, they start to resent you because you don't know who they are. Or more importantly, they feel they aren't allowed to be what they really want to be, or who they really are because of you. It's not guidance, that's control, and not in a good way. So, to guide our children, we have to teach them how to figure it out and think for themselves. To do for self and not wait for someone to come and do everything for them. We have to learn how to help, which is our H word that works hand in hand with guidance.

Chapter H

H *is for*
Help

H is for help. Help can be done in various ways for various reasons. It is our job to recognize what type of help our children need sometimes, even if they don't ask for it. When we are guiding, we are helping to a certain extent. The thing about help, just like guidance, it could be to show or direct. Other times it could be to do for them. The problem lies again, in when we do it too often. Just like in guidance, when we are helping our children and we do too much for them, we are hindering them, not helping them. Again, balance is key. We have to balance where it comes into play. When, in some cases, are we helping too much? In others, when are we not helping enough? Now I know you like oh come on Ms. J, I'm confused! Am I supposed to help or not? Am I supposed to guide or not? Which is it?! Unfortunately, the answer doesn't lie in one or the other because it is in both.

The question is not how but when. When to guide and when to help. My answer for that would be as needed. Keyword here NEED. I didn't say as wanted. I said as needed. It comes with putting the needs of the child before yours. When I say this, I mean because THEY ARE ready and not because YOU AREN'T or refuse to see it. I'm going to take it a step further and say, you only step in after they have honestly tried without succeeding. I know a lot of you may be like, "what?!" So let me give you some examples of what I am saying. A child needs help putting their shoes on. You say, "Okay, after you try first", let them sincerely try with real effort. If they are unsuccessful, then you provide help by explaining and showing how to do it. You repeat this until they learn how to successfully put their shoes on. A child needs help opening a bag of chips. You ask "did you try first?" For the most part, if they want those chips, they gone learn how to open that bag, you don't have to worry about that. But, we want them to do it in a more non messy way. Show them how it's done the correct way and continue to do this until they successfully know how. What about that toddler who turned 2 and wants to do everything on their own? Let them, but also monitor them in the process. If it's for safety reasons, guide, or be close enough to step in at any moment. What about the child that needs help and doesn't want to ask for some, or too afraid to ask? Depending on the situation it is up to you to figure it out and help anyway. Just make sure you have a conversation with them about speaking up and asking for help afterwards. Or you could say nothing at all. You could do it indirectly or directly, it's all up to you and depends on the situation. A baby at school messing with your child and he or she doesn't say anything or want you to know. Maybe that's a situation you handle indirectly. Your child is a great child, helps around the house, does good in school, has a job and is saving for something big they want and you think he deserves it. They are $100 short. Help them out. It's a level of balance to these situations and everything that we do. Because doing that last example for a child that doesn't work, doesn't help, and is entitled I wouldn't suggest you buy them anything or do nothing for them. Because then that turns into hindering and not helping. It could also turn into a bigger problem depending on the situation. You may now be creating a monster.

What about that child who gets asked important questions by individuals, and when you are around, you do all the answering for them? He or she doesn't even get a chance to speak. That's not help, that's hindrance, control, and hella annoying!! Do you understand, all in all, what I'm getting at here with guidance and help? There is a fine line between guiding and helping, doing and hindering. You must be aware. The best way to approach the situation when guiding or helping your children is to ask yourself this every time. What if something bad happens to me tomorrow? I fall out and need emergency assistance. Have I given my child or even students enough tools, lessons, guidance, instruction for them to help themselves and figure it out on their own? To get me help? If your answer is no, then you're hindering them and doing too much for them. Start teaching through guidance more, letting them learn to think for themselves more and figure it out. Work with them and not for them. This alone can make or break the type of bond you will have with your child, and even students. It can be a healthy one, or an unhealthy one.

Chapter I

I *is for*
Interest, Independence, Inspire & Instruct

Let's start with interest. The question will be, do you know your child or student's interest? Are you supportive of them? Support is the backing of someone or something even when there is nothing for you to gain from it. In this case though, it is something to gain when you support your children or students' interest. It is a bond, a new level of understanding, and a peek into their mind. Awesome, right? Just consider how it makes you feel when your significant other supports or learns more about your interests, or your dreams. Better yet, they get involved with it, even if it isn't what they like or intended to do for themselves. It's a turn on, right? You feel loved. It makes you happy. It's a pleasant surprise. It makes you appreciate their willingness to learn a little bit more about why you love something so much, right? You also feel a little bit closer when it's all said and done. Am I Right? The same thing goes for children (except the turn on part that was strictly for the adults). They are surprised, excited, happy and feel like you care and appreciate them. They are appreciative of your support of their interests. As we discussed in Chapter E, it is important to engage. Interact with your children. Don't be a bump on the log. You gotta get up, get out and do something with them. When you incorporate yourself into their interests, it's easier to do that, or find things to do that will help you interact and engage with them more. When you do learn about their interests or things they like, I would also encourage you to participate in them as well. Now I know you may be thinking "well engage and participate are the same," but they are slightly different.

But, we will talk more in detail about participation later. For now, we are focusing on interest.

I want you to remember to show your interest by engaging and participating. It does wonders for the relationship, and it teaches you so much about your child. The best part is, those moments get cherished the most, even when you do it for older children and adults. I think as we get older, we start to slack in these areas with our older children and even our significant others sometimes. That creates a space or a void to be filled by someone or something else. Think about it, aren't we always drawn to people with similar interests? Then, when it comes to those who don't have similar interests, we only become closer in our differences because we are willing to learn a little more about each other. When people don't want to learn about us, our passion, purpose, goals etc. We start to create distance, whether subconsciously or not. Why does this happen? It's simply because "we" don't think "you" care, so why bother right? Annnnnd that is exactly what your children are thinking when you don't show some type of interest in things they are interested in. "Why bother?" "You don't care anyway." Bam! And just like that, it starts to create distance. Which is the opposite of what you want to do when trying to strengthen a bond or connection. This is the dynamic I see mostly with older students, starting as young as 3rd and 4th grade, parents are not interested in their interests. Not even aware. Then out of nowhere, it seems the children are subjected to a lot of other things, especially if they live in hood areas. Those innocent interests now turn into something else without you realizing it. Like joining gangs, pregnancy or other things. You being supportive of something they like to do earlier on, can help you guide them into the direction they should go. Showing interest for the things they are interested in, goes deeper than creating a bond, it can be life changing.

That leads me to my next I, inspire. Inspire children to be more and to even be better than you. Leading by example works with this. But you also have to often send out words of encouragement for all things. Build confidence in that child. See quiet as kept, everything discussed in his book will build up your child's confidence in themselves if you do it. I know because I do these things with every student I have ever taught, and it works. I'm not telling you to take my word for it. I'm telling you to try all things discussed in this book and see for yourself. When I am around children or teaching them. I don't ever want them to feel like there is something they can't do. Yes, we have to tread lightly with certain words when they are younger, (because young children are very literal), but you don't only have to use words to inspire. You can use pictures, clothes, stories, anything. Most importantly, you can put that of which they inspire to be, right in front of them. What do I mean by this, your child wants to be a ballerina, encourage them! Take them to the ballet. Let them see Misty Copeland. Can't afford the ballet, go buy you and your child some tutus, and ballerina shoes and tip toe around the damn house! The same goes for our sons! Especially them! They want to be an archeologist and you don't know anybody, you better go to the store and buy some paint brushes and go play in the dirt! Let's not make excuses as to why we can't inspire or be an inspiration to our children, when it's that simple.

Let's continue. Instruct. I'm not going to stay on this too long, because it is the same as guidance. And help. Same rules apply. I will add that it is on us adults to do this and break it down step by step for the children so they can learn. When we instruct, not only are we giving knowledge, we are training. A lot of times we don't want to break anything down. We just expect them to know. That is not instruction. YOU waste time by not breaking it down first, in the first place. You will have to have a lot of patience when you instruct, because learning can take time. Not everyone is a fast learner. When you don't instruct properly, you risk the possibility of that child shutting down. Combine guidance, help, and patience with what we discussed in chapter D with discipline and we got a hit! It works. As we move along, you will notice a lot of the chapters coincide with one another. You have to do a lot of what I am talking about together while teaching children. When you do, it works wonders.

Last but not least, independence. We have to help our children be independent from us. What do I mean by that? Simple, let them be themselves and find out who they are. Let them practice things and do things on their own. Let them be free from your control sometimes. This is something I think my dad did his best to keep a good balance with. But I also had so much responsibility on me at a young age, I think if he didn't let me have dramatic outbursts (because that's what it was haha, yea it got kinda crazy in the house), and have my free time, I may have turned out different.

My dad has this saying. "My house. My rules." I didn't like most of the rules in his house of course. (Til this day, I still don't) I couldn't wait to leave! But because guidance and discipline was in the house as well as a level of independence, when I left, I didn't wild out. As I grew to discover more of my voice and what I wanted, each year I learned something new about those rules and why they were there. Could this have gone a different way if there was no discipline and guidance in the house and just independence? Absolutely. We see it all the time. Children out here, are too independent with no guidance running the streets, catching STIs at young ages, or getting into trouble. Could it have gone another way if my dad let me have too much guidance and discipline in the house and no independence whatsoever, before I left to go to college? I would say so. I believe I would have become even more rebellious (yes I'm a rebel with a cause) and ended up getting myself into trouble. But ehh, I'm great, a force to be reckoned with. So hey, I guess his balance plan worked.

See my dad raised us to think for ourselves, my mom too, so therefore it's their fault I'm so independent in the first place. Ha! We also had to be prepared to live, in case something happened to them. With an independent person at a young age, I believe you have to give them guidance and discipline or they will wild out. Of course, this is not a one size fits all here. I'm just trying to give parents a new perspective. Too often I see children turn out to be the opposite of what the parent(s) wanted, with too little or too much independence. Simply because discipline and guidance or both are often left out. You do have to have a level of balance in giving them the opportunity to be themselves and figure it out.

I work with and talk to children, especially older children who have no level of independence and feel stuck. Trapped. It's like they are in jail in their own home. Is that what we want for them? To feel like that, and get so used to those feelings, that if they end up going down the wrong path, God forbid, and end up in jail for real, there is a level of comfort there. Because they know that feeling all too well? The children who weren't allowed to experience anything, in my experience, are the ones who can't think for themselves at all. You ask them a question about how they feel, they be like, "I don't know, let me ask my mama." I get so annoyed, it's like you can't have a conversation with them, because they don't know who they are. They've never done anything or had conversations about anything, so when they go off to college they want to try everything! I have talked to grownups who have never once done what they wanted to do for themselves, following in the footsteps of their parents because they had no other choice. Or at least felt that way, and is now miserable. They're holding on to past childhood trauma, not realizing they have the power to do or be whatever they want. We should not strip opportunity from our children to find their voice amongst the crowd. You can't, not guide, not help and not allow some independence. That's a recipe for disaster.

The topic of independence is always a tricky one when I talk to parents. They are always like…"ummm I don't know"… For some parents, when we start to talk about independence, the topic of Will Smith and Jada's kids Jaden and Willow always come up. (They always forget about Trey tho) They always use them as an example of what "too much independence" looks like. They be like, "I don't want that for my children". And I was thinking, "you don't want smart children?" "Children who think for themselves?" "Can make a decision on their own?" "Who would be financially stable if you were to die?" "Who can speak up for themselves?" "Who don't care what other people think?" "Jaden doesn't have 50 baby mamas and not taking care of his children, neither does Trey and Willow ain't out here hoe'n." Not that I know of. We don't have to agree on parenting style or whatever, but to me, those are some smart kids! Well young adults. I don't know how old they are, but I know they are younger than me. I think Will and Jada did a great job with balancing their independence. In my experience, that's not what a bad look of "too much independence" looks like. I gave my example of what too much independence with the lack of discipline and guidance looks like to me when I see or experience it from children. Trust they are not Willows or Jadens! I don't look at independence so much as an image thing, because I think that's where people get caught up on and focus on the most, when we talk about independence. Independence to me is almost a survival mechanism, and we have to have it! Think about it whenever you are not sure. Ask yourself this question or better yet, ask your child or student this question. "Do you feel like I don't allow you time to figure it out or be yourself?" From there have a genuine and candid discussion from that. The answer will let you know what to do.

Chapter J

J *is for*
Justify

J is for justify, I know, sounds weird. I thought so too. But I needed a strong word for J. This word will work hand in hand with candid conversation and letting children speak. Oftentimes as teachers or parents, when setting rules or boundaries, some of it we can't justify. You know how I know, because your favorite go to is "because I said so." I laugh as I write this because it is wrong on so many levels. How do we expect them to understand anything and be okay with what we are saying if we can't justify our own actions? If a child is sincerely confused or really doesn't understand your actions, why not explain? And to make it worse, we don't allow them to justify theirs. I'm not gonna lie. It's funny sometimes. Because it absolutely makes no sense. We can at least hear each other out. The things we say or do sometimes… And a lot of times it's because the real answer is, we don't want to put in the work, or have the conversation, or let go of control. It can even be because we ourselves really don't know, Ha! So, because we don't have a justifiable reason, we use that "saying" because it's all we know. We have a hard time justifying our actions sometimes, because in all actuality we can't. Same goes for our children. How do we fix this? By being honest, by being real, not only to ourselves, but with each other. We have to hold each other accountable. When that child does something or wants to do something you don't necessarily agree with, talk about it. Reason with one another. Make sure your actions and decisions are justifiable. There's already too much injustice going on in the world. Let's not bring it into our homes.

Chapter K

K *is for*
Knowledge of Self

K is for knowledge of self. This one right here. Buckle up because it's going to be a bumpy ride. For all those reading this, get ready to either be held accountable, hear some harsh truth and or have a whole range of emotion come about. Forewarning, this part is especially for my people! I want y'all to listen! Other cultures, I want y'all to listen as well, but with a different ear. Because I believe it is something we all have to fix. The only question I have for myself is where to start. Yeesh! Knowledge of self goes beyond who you are on the inside and what you look like on the outside. Some people may not agree with this, but knowledge of self even goes as far as knowing your family history and knowing your culture and historical background.

I have some friends that think that type of knowledge isn't important. Or used to think that way. We would argue all the time about it. Here's why. I believe if you don't know your history or background it will repeat itself. Marcus Garvey once said, "A people without the knowledge of their past history is like a tree without roots". Maya Angelou once said, "you can't really know where you're going until you know where you have been." Then you have the philosopher George Santayana, who said, "Those who do not remember the past are condemned to repeat it." He's also the person who said "a child educated only at school is an uneducated child."

All of these quotes are of something in which I believe. "Why?" you ask. I see some bits and examples of all of this every day. Our children are lost. They don't know who they are, let alone their parents. Half of them come from a single-parent home not knowing who their dad is. Most of the time, unaware of the history of their immediate family, let alone the history of the people in their culture. Our homes are broken. If you understood the history of the past, you would know that IT was always the plan to keep the homes broken. And maybe if you knew, you would fight more, or strive more not to break up the Black family dynamic. During slavery, they bred us, and then sold us off. This is what some people do to dogs. It is viewed as completely inappropriate for that to be done to dogs, but they felt it was right to do it to Africans. Then as time went along, the Black family Dynamic gets stronger, what new system gets put into place for struggling Blacks, welfare. I'll give the woman money, the man has to leave the home. What sense does that make?! None! That's why it was done. Let's make it harder for the Black man to make a living, then let's put cocaine on the streets, allow them to sell it to make money, find them, then send them to jail. While simultaneously killing their communities! I'm paraphrasing everything, because we all know this alone can be 50 books. But the point I'm trying to make here is, if you think children understood this, learned about the TRUTH of how this system works against them in school, do you think that they would still allow it to happen? Of course not! That's why the real United States history isn't being taught in schools anymore. Therefore, YOU the parent must teach it! SO THEY KNOW, and historical mistakes can stop, or at least be slowed down.

The history lesson doesn't stop there, you as parents, need to talk about yourself. Parents don't talk about themselves or how it was for them growing up. Why is that? Do your children even know you? The real question is, do you want your children to know you? You've changed now…well how so? Please elaborate. Do your children know some embarrassing moments you've had? Mistakes you've made, the lessons you learned? No. You don't talk about that. You just bark orders and pay bills. No time for learning and teaching. Then you send them to schools that don't tell the truth about America, or any other culture. They just talk about Caucasians who supposedly do so many awesome things for this country. They breeze past smallpox and lining the roads with trails of tears. The country that was built on the backs of African Americans who were stolen from another country. Almost all the great inventions were done by African Americans, but our children know nothing of how wonderful their minds are or that their ancestors built something as simple as the street lights they look at every day. They don't talk about how we treat our neighbors in Canada and Mexico like there's something wrong with them. But use their work ethic for cheap labor and minimum wages. Hell, the children don't even know that Puerto Rico is an incorporated territory of the United States and they damn sure don't know that the country they live in is a big ass business. Why? Because they are not teaching that in school. What are they teaching? I am a teacher, and I still believe a lot of things taught in school, especially as the children get older, is a bunch of bullshit. My question for parents and teachers alike. Are we molding our children or guiding them? And which do you think is better?

Let's start with the definition of molding. Molding, "a decorative recessed or relief surface. To mold is to knead or work into a design, or a desired consistent neat shape. It can also mean to determine or influence the quality or nature of." Now let's go to guide, to guide is "to advise." "Assure the way to others. To direct or have an influence on the course of action." Now before I tie all this together, let me say we do too much molding instead of guiding. I believe to guide is much more important than to mold. Why? Because the day I was born, I was molded. I don't need anyone else trying to mold me into something different, but rather guide or help me understand the life given that I'm living so that I can fulfill my purpose. You have people out here, re-molding the God given image they received at birth! Why?! You were already perfectly made.

Now it's just a bunch of plastic barbie dolls in human form running around. I don't understand it. But maybe, just maybe, if we knew how great we were, we wouldn't feel the need to change anything about our bodies or ourselves! History has told us, our skin is different, therefore we are ugly and not made beautifully in his image! I don't know about y'all, but baby I AM THE IMAGE!!! That is what we should be teaching our children! We are not teaching them to love themselves, we are teaching them to love the mold of someone else.

When you guide me, you influence the decision. But at the end of the day, it is my choice. When you guide, you show me which way to go. Allow me to learn from you and your mistakes. But also from my own. When you guide you advise, and when you mold we don't get much of a choice, right. Apply that thought process to what is going on with the children! I mean, when I was born, I didn't get to pick my birth date, weight, height, year I was born, nothing. I was made in His image. I was molded in his image. Let me ask you this. When you are molding your children, whose image are they made in? Is it yours or his? When you send them to school, what image is that school trying to portray? Do you see where I'm going with this here? If you are confused right now with all my questions, this is how I teach, by asking questions. Right now I want you to think. I sincerely want you to answer that question. Whose image are you molding your child into? What image is the school molding your child into? Now answer this. Who is your child? Are they being themselves or the image that someone else wants them to be? Ms. J What does this have to do with knowledge of self? History and cultural awareness? EVERYTHING!

One it's bad enough as a black woman, I can say that in the wrong work environment, I can't even be myself without it being a problem. If I'm grown and feel that way, imagine how the youth feel in these schools that are telling half truths, making our children feel bad for being themselves. Imagine what they are going through. "Your skin is too dark." "You don't speak proper English." "you're too tall." "You're too skinny." "You're too fat." "You're too light" "Your eyebrows too thick." "Why yo daddy don't ever come around?" "Why yo mama look like that?" Why why why? And I'm not gone act like I wasn't a person who made colorism jokes as a child or talked about someone every now and again, because we all do. But, at the very least I knew when it happened to me, being talked about, or called out my name, it could roll off my shoulders. I knew who I was, and did not care about what people said about me. I also knew my history and where I came from. So those words did not bother me. But all children are not like that. If you don't tell them at a young age, why their dark skin is special, and why their accent is unique, and why it's dope that they can speak another language, society will tear them down.

When children know their background, they could be proud of their heritage, not letting anyone knock them off their game. When children are aware of their family background, it can lead to an explanation of why they experienced some unknown or unexpected behaviors. It can also give a deeper understanding of where they came from. "That attitude you got, came from your mama. That running from responsibility came from yo daddy, he used to do that all the time. You have frequent seizures and out bursts, schizophrenia runs in the family. Yo uncle and a couple of cousins had that too. You're trying to fix it? Here's what helped us." Being aware of past traumas can help your child overcome theirs or steer clear of it all together. It could give them understanding so they can move forward with a better mindset. Even knowing about family disease and health issues can help you better know what to eat to be healthier. Children knowing their parents a little better, helps them to understand themselves a little better. Uncover hidden agendas behind rules, and also their parents. More importantly, build a better relationship.

Schools are not guiding anymore. It's a business, a backwards ass business at that. Too many times I'm talking to children who are involved with gangs because they feel like those gangs are their family. They know about the gang's history more than they know about theirs. I know children who speak another language at home, but don't want to speak it at school. Even worse. I know individuals who don't want to learn to speak their native language even though they have someone in a home speaking the language. They would prefer to speak English and forget their language altogether. I've met parents who are from other countries, who change their child's name for the sake of having an American name. (rolls eyes) I'm calling these babies names and they are not answering because it's not their name!! I am always explaining to other cultures that it is my responsibility to learn how to say your name correctly! What you are doing isn't helping the child! At least not with me. Be proud of what you named your child. Allow your child to be proud of their name! And I'm not even gone start on you negros who say, "Nu uh, I want my baby to have a white name so they can get them a good job." As I type this, I'm like, you know what… (with that look on my face, y'all know what look I'm talking about)….that's a book for another day. Just know, people like you, get on my nerves. Let me say something to all my parents who have unique names that people consider "ghetto". Girl, if ain't nobody else told you! Let me be the first! AIN'T NOTHING WRONG WITH YO BABY NAME! And if you are worried about him or her getting a job, send them to me! I got you! Better yet, let them start their own business and hire the Ashley's, the Brittneys, the Michaels, and the Toms! I see nothing wrong with our children having names that have meanings behind them! That's how it's supposed to be! And if your baby's name is the mama and the daddy's name mixed together, that's ok!!

Just make sure your baby knows the history of Mommy and Daddy is all I'm saying!

Let me keep it moving, 'cause as y'all can see I'm over here a lil hot! But before I move on, let me say this, no shade to people with the "regular names", especially the Michaels. I have a brother named Michael. But what y'all gone stop doing is throwing shade to the Zamoras because you think it's ghetto. Better yet because yo ass don't know how to sound out words! Looka here baby! My family is filled with "ghetto" names and I love it! I love my name. I like being different and my name having meaning! I have a friend I have never met before on Facebook who's sole purpose of our friendship is because we have the same name. I have never met her. She's from Nigeria. She asked to be my friend and because my page is private, when I saw her name I said "yup!" She said she had never met or seen anyone else with our name ever, and I hadn't either. I asked her if it had a meaning and she said "yeah, treasure." And I was like "I knew I was priceless!" I said, "that's why whenever anybody would ask me what my name meant I would say unique, cause I'm different." She said, "we certainly are." And we laughed. We are still friends on Facebook till this day. But you all just don't know what that little moment meant for me! Growing up, it wasn't no finding my name on a keychain or license plate at the souvenir store, not even my nickname. (It may be a small possibility now, my nickname is being used in movies more! Shout out to Ninja Assasin for being the first and Coming to America 2, for being the second!! Main characters too, that's what I'm talking about. And they were both Black so they had the right association with the name HA!) I did know how my name came about, which adds to the story of me being unique. I was my mama's Nika. (It's some more to the story, but that's all yall getting) So thank you mama and I don't know if she will ever read this book, but Minika Edem thank you as well! I will always have a special place for you in my heart for that!

Getting back on topic, children are hating their skin tones, names, body and themselves. No one is telling them that they are beautiful, handsome, smart, or speaking affirmations over them at home. I come across so many students who don't have their own identity. They are either living the life that their parents want them to live or they completely don't have a clue what they want at all. So afraid to speak up and step out, and do what it is they want to do for themselves. It even affects them when they get older. As teachers we should know and do better. Why sit back and continue to teach lies because it's in the curriculum? Not allowing our students to know the truth. Not allowing them to be themselves. Not teaching them how to critically think for themselves. Not being supportive of their goals and guiding them as best we can and in the direction that will help them to succeed at accomplishing that goal.

I can't lie. I always felt like child care could be done better, that's why I wanted to start my own. Another big reason that keeps me aiming for that goal is, because when I do good, set standards and my students supersede expectations, I have a target on my back. When I don't tolerate mistreatment of myself or my students, I then become an angry black woman who is deemed as a threat or insubordinate. What's crazy is yes, these moments mostly come from working in all-white establishments, but it hurts even more when it comes while working with African American ones. It's even worse in my opinion. You mean to tell me you want me to have to feel like I'm not good enough everywhere I go? Then when I know I'm doing good and right, I gotta dumb it down? I can't do exceptional work? Because a person who doesn't want to put in the work feels threatened by my work? What sense does that make? I never felt threatened by another good teacher! I took that as an opportunity to learn! Hell, teach me! Let me pick up some tips. It has always baffled me when I work somewhere and am told that I am teaching too much and told not only what to teach, but how as well. And that is where I draw the line, because that just does not work for me.

I can remember the most disappointing day in my career working at a childcare center in Illinois. My students were learning. The parents were happy, I mean their children were superseding milestones that their parents didn't even know they could! I decided to have fun with my class one day and we did the cha cha slide, which is educational as well. Teaches left from right, hand and eye coordination, balance and a good source of exercise. A white parent whose child attended the school complained. She didn't want her child listening to "hip hop". Crazy part was, that child wasn't even in my class! Ha! Now I'm brought into the office to not only be warned to not listen to the cha cha slide again, because it's "inappropriate" but to be told that I had to stop teaching my students. Ha ha ha, y'all I can't make this shit up! The owner and the director of the center was a Black woman. So I was thoroughly confused. Me being me, I had to have a heart to heart with her, on some real shit. Because she knew my goals. I could not understand why all of the sudden this was happening, when she was ecstatic a few weeks ago about what I was doing! Happy about the students' progress and the parents' praise! I said "hey there is nothing inappropriate about the cha cha slide and you know it. We listen to every other cultures' music here, and I don't even speak Spanish. That music can be saying anything and we wouldn't know. Now what our people listen to is inappropriate because a white parent doesn't like it?" I said, "You are the owner! You Black, tell her if she doesn't like it to take her child somewhere else." She told me no, she couldn't do that and it's just some things I didn't understand. I'm thinking to myself, you damn right! I shol' don't understand. Then I asked her why I gotta "stop teaching so much", and she said to me y'all, and I bullshit you not. She said, "what they gone learn when they get to the yellow room?" (that was the name of the other class) And I was like, "sh a lot! For starters, how to read! What you mean?!" I was then told that the teachers in the other room weren't as good as me, and I was doing what they are currently teaching their class, (which were 4 and 5 year olds) so I'mma have to calm it down. I just looked at her. All respect for her went out the window, and I said to myself, I refuse. I kept wondering if she was serious. She was dead serious. They ended up going through a play base accreditation, and with that, all of the sudden I couldn't teach anything anymore. The children just had to be there and play all day, like I was babysitting. They kept coming into my room to make sure of it, so I quit. Since then, that has been a repetitive process of my life when working at these establishments. They want you to teach what they want, nothing more, nothing less. And when you do too good a job, they find a way to either get you out or make your life so miserable that you don't want to be there anymore. This is why my resume looks the way it does and I don't care. This is also why the school systems are failing. Because if you teach the children too well, who's gonna teach them after you? "No you teaching to much, dumb it down, because the teachers they are going to next aren't as good." That's what 95% of the school systems are made of now. It's not just me. I notice how often that other strong willed and like minded, good ass teachers go through the same thing for doing what's right. For teaching what's right. It's not a school that I have worked at, where I can say that I have not seen that type of treatment happen to good teachers. Who stood up for themselves, taught the kids well, and was the bomb, but was treated like shit. I have not seen the opposite yet, and have been working in the field for over 15 years. So not only do I want to create a space for myself, but for those teachers and students as well. So they can finally see and understand how important it is to know thyself. Staying true to themselves and proud of their history, culture and family, no matter how much ugliness the world portrays.

Knowledge of self is key. Because if you don't have it, you won't ever know how important you are. How wonderful and magnificent you are. You won't be able to stand in your truth and in your power! You will start to do any and everything for a little change, when you can truly be making big dollars. Accepting who you are starts in the mind, yes. But if your mind is shaped and molded wrong in the beginning, it will be harder to come undone. That's why setting that foundation for your child in the beginning is SO IMPORTANT! Fredrick Douglas said it best. "It is easier to build strong children, than to repair broken men." Teaching that starts at home because most school systems mold and not guide. They are not set up to help your children discover who they are and their purpose in life. Maybe in the past it was, but now it's almost like it's free babysitting at some of these schools. If you don't pour into your children at home, suffer the consequences of that child possibly not knowing just how important his or her life is. We don't want traumatic family history and experiences to repeat itself. Fucked up USA history to repeat itself, our history of bad health and eating habits to repeat itself. All that changes by guiding, knowing when to and how to is key. But most importantly all that changes with knowledge, and being knowledgeable of your history.

Chapter L

L *is for*
Listen & Love

L is for love and listen. Everything we do should be with love. Everything. When I was in undergrad, I learned that there were seven different types of love. I got older and argued with a dude who felt like First Corinthians 13 4-8 was the only definition and type of love, and that there were no other types of love in the bible. When I kindly told him he was wrong, he couldn't understand, and of course he wanted me to prove it. So I read him Romans 12 9-21. So now it's an inside joke between me and him. He Corinthians me and I Romans him. Our argument started because he felt love is the same for everyone, and I felt differently. I agreed that we should love one another, but the way in which I love my mother and father may be different in the way I love my sister and brother. Then that love would be different in the way I love my husband or boyfriend, from the way I love my child. I was saying there are different types of love, but he was saying it wasn't, until Romans. He probably still feels different, but that's fine. With that being said we all have different types of love languages. Do you know your child's? For the most part, most children at a very young age will signify love with time. The time you invest into them usually amounts to how much you love them. Yea the gifts and things may seem ok at first, but if you are never around it gets old. In a world where time just seems like it's never enough. How do you let a child know that you love them without saying it? Well, I believe for the most part, you do everything we have already discussed in chapters A through K, and continue to do those things we discuss from L to Z. Say it, show it, do it, prove it, (and if you did not go back and sing that part, we can't be friends). Just like that Blackstone song says, you have to put in the work. Love is a verb. But in all seriousness, be there the best way you can and for the simple things, because usually that's what means the most. Sometimes children don't feel loved because most things discussed between A and K have not or are not being done.

The next biggest thing that can affect the way your child feels or views love from you is the notion of you listening. Are you even listening to them? Do you hear them when they talk to you? Or does it go in one ear and out the other? Does what they have to say matters? I encourage you to listen to your child with intent. It is knowledge in what they do or don't say. When you really listen to your child it can teach you a lot about them. How or what they think. How or what they feel. If they do or don't think. Why they do or don't think the way they do, or what they do or don't know. Do they comprehend the lessons you teach? Do they understand things from different perspectives? Are you understanding of their perspective?

More importantly, what they do or don't say when you are having a conversation with them matters tremendously. It could tell you if they are nervous, afraid, hurt, scared, ashamed, embarrassed, happy, remorseful, confident or not. It could tell you many things, but you will miss it. You will miss it all, if you don't listen to what is said. If you don't listen, when you interact, discipline, challenge, engage, help or guide, you might miss something you can better address or fix. You have to listen to your child in all ways. Especially when you give them the floor to express themselves and voice their opinions and views. When you all are having candid conversations, don't be so quick to dismiss what they are saying. You may miss something very important. Listening to your child in many cases can save their life if they are going through something. I urge parents and teachers to really start listening to the children. It matters.

Chapter M

M *is for*
Mistake & Motivate

M is for mistakes and motivate. Well as you know, or should know, children make mistakes from the time they start flipping over and trying to move. If we as adults understand making mistakes is what helps you to learn, why don't we understand the same things for children? In fact, at least for me, I am more susceptible to children's mistakes than adults. Like it drives me crazy when we adults keep making the same mistakes over and over again as if we don't have the knowledge or understanding to know when something is or isn't right or wrong. Then turn around and act as if someone who hasn't been on this earth for longer than five years could understand what we can't even understand in our twenty, thirty, or 45 years of existence. Isn't that crazy? This upsets me when I see adults coming down on children for mistakes, especially when they are making the same mistakes! They are learning it from you! This is why it is easier for me to look over a child's mistake and not get so up in arms about it. But for adults, I still have to remind myself that we did not grow up the same, experience the same, learn the same way or do the same things. Therefore, I'm learning how to give adults more grace and understanding. And I must say, it is tremendously hard for me. (Especially since I don't like people. I love yall, I don't like you) I say all this to help you understand, that children are going to constantly make mistakes. It is how they learn. How you address those mistakes with them will make or break if they could turn to you or not when they make them. See I don't necessarily want adults to turn to me when they make a mistake (unless it's in a workplace). But, I want a child to feel like they can and be able to come to me if they made a mistake. The difference is primarily because I feel like you're an adult, you should know better. Again, that's something I'm working on. Plus, I think from a more proactive standpoint. So, I would rather help the adult before the mistakes happen. But for children, it's the complete opposite. In fact, for children, I don't even want to be proactive as much, especially when they are younger. Yea for areas of safety, of course, but for discovery, no. If they are discovering and being curious or trying to figure something out, (that's safe of course) the lesson usually comes after the mistake. I may step in and correct them afterward and then I want to see how they grow from it.

Because I have this frame of mind when children make mistakes, I'm not so bothered by it. I understand that they are going to make mistakes. Mistakes are going to happen! So, when it happens, especially for the first time, I'm not mad, angry or disgruntled. I can talk and approach the situation in a calm manner, or a firm matter, depending on the situation. Not cussing them out, making them feel less than, or most importantly not making them feel like they can't come to me. Because if they don't want to come to me when mistakes are made, it'll be a lot harder to teach them. It will also be a lot harder to keep them from continuing to make the same mistake or similar mistakes in the future. When children make mistakes, like with everything else, we have to embrace the process. Now, as a grown adult, I have just learned how to embrace the process. Last year, I literally just accepted embracing the process in 2021. Looking at it from a different perspective for myself. Maybe it was because when I was younger, I felt like mistakes were unacceptable. My dad used to have this saying, "do it right the first time so you won't have to do it over." Therefore, I constantly want to do things right the first time so I won't have to do it over. That has been my frame of mind. It has taken the majority of my life to learn and understand making mistakes is okay. Not to be so hard on myself. What's funny is deep down inside, I probably already knew that, because when working with children, I never came down on them the way my dad came down on me, because I understood they have to learn and it's okay. Ultimately that's what I am here for, to guide them through the process.

When making mistakes and embracing our process, we have to expect the children to be children. Part of that is knowing that mistakes are coming, and are going to happen. Be prepared for it. Help yourself be proactive and not reactive when it comes to this part of your child's learning phase. What do I mean by that? For example, if I am getting ready to do a project in class that I know children are going to be excited about, I expect some mistakes to happen. Why? Because of the excitement. Things like their behavior is going to change as well. So instead of getting upset, when it is happening, or when it does happen, I prepare for it. As much as possible. How? Well one, me and the children sit down and we have a conversation about the project. We go over the rules and how it will go. If it is messy, I expect some messes from the children. They may even argue over some of the choices. So I set it up in a certain way ahead of time to minimize those messes, and the arguments. I also prepare for their listening to not be so great. I understand at the moment, they have tunnel vision and they only care about that one thing until it is over. Because of that they may act out a couple of times in class. They may even act out at home because the project is all they can think about. "I'm so excited!" "I can't wait to get started." Or "But I didn't finish my project. Oh my goodness. I can't wait until my project is done." So now I have to warn the parents. That's part of being proactive too. "Hey, we have this exciting project coming up. Your child's behavior may change at home because of the excitement, but don't worry, we have it under control. If their behavior gets out of control, just continue to redirect them to what it is that you want them to do or learn. Bring their focus back on the assignment at hand and continue to change the subject. That is how you stay clear of tantrums and things of that nature until the project is done." Now because I have this knowledge of the excitement, due to the project, if something were to happen in class, I don't have to worry their parents about stories of they're "not so good behavior". In those moments, I address it with the children and give them the opportunity to change it as well.

Understanding children's behavior and how mistakes happen when they are excited helps me to be a little bit more prepared. Understanding that when children are excited sometimes, they can't contain or control it, and mistakes happen, helps me not to be upset when something small does happen. I understand it is not intentional. They're just excited. So, no need for me to scream, curse, belittle or get mad at anything. Remember, this method of helping during mistakes doesn't just apply to excitement. It could be applied to mistakes they make when they are confused, scared, angry and hurt as well. At the end of the day, I want them to work through mistakes and be better, and if anything, this is a chance for me to help motivate them to do just that.

Motivate? Why is it important to motivate your children? Let me ask you this, have you ever met an unmotivated person? I have, they are lazy and don't want to do anything. They don't even want to try half of the time. Not being willing to try is the death to learning, growing or getting better at anything. We want our children to learn. Most importantly, we want them to WANT to learn! When you encourage them to do better, be better, try harder, that's a form of motivation. Speaking over them with good intentions and wanting them to succeed is key. Speak to them in a manner that lets them know it is okay to try again. That, "Don't give up" needs to be heard, trust me it matters. It does something to their confidence as well. With that being said, I encourage you to always speak life into your children and not death.

Chapter N

N *is for*
No

    N is for no, I want you guys to know that it is okay to say no to your children. I'm not sure at what point you all stop telling them no, because it's usually a toddlers first word. But some of you don't just don't tell your child no enough. You spoil them, give them everything they want. Then they come out into a world feeling entitled. Yes, I said it. They are out here entitled than a mug. Now they don't know how to act when they hear the word no. For some it leads to behavior problems. I hate to say it but hearing 'no' more than 'yes' builds up a sense of resilience, builds character and determination. Yet, just like everything else in this book, telling children no has to come with a level of balance. We don't want to discourage them and it shouldn't seem like we don't support them. When and when not to tell them no, is everything. The whole goal here is, not to spoil your child so much that when they don't get their way they don't know how to act. They don't know how to adapt, or they shut down. They don't want to keep moving forward or try again. That is not what we want. I want you to at least say no enough, that when they hear it, they are so determined to get a yes, they figure out how to flip that no into a yes. Yet also know when no means no. The challenge for you as an adult is saying no, meaning it and standing on it. Like if it's something that's a sincere no, that is not a time to try to be your child's friend. Your student's friend. No compromising. There is a lesson to be learned. Say what you mean and mean what you say, so they can know. They have to understand that they can't pull one over on you. They also have to know when you're being serious. If there is an opportunity for them to change that no into a yes, it has to come in a form of compromise, or negotiation. Maybe you choose to give it through options or choices. I'm not sure when you should, because it always depends on certain circumstances. But do not be that teacher who says no then turn around right after you say no, and give the child exactly what they want. They will know that no doesn't really mean no when it comes to you. Therefore, if they keep being annoying in the worst way, just a little bit longer, they can get whatever they want.

Yet, that same example can also be a good thing, if they are really serious about something they really want. Whether it's a life goal or a toy. It can speak of resilience. The question then becomes, what is the end goal here? That is why when and when not to tell them no, means so much more. The lesson is behind the reason for the no. Which makes how they handle hearing no, that much more important. How are they reacting? Are they standing tall and constantly moving forward with a positive, yet clever attitude? Or is it, scream, holler, beg, complain, cry and act a plum fool, til' I get what I want? How will this translate into their lives as they grow and get older? That is the question, and also why we shouldn't feel bad about telling them no at times.

Chapter O

O *is for*
Options & Observe

O is for options and observe. We talked about options a little earlier in Chapter C. We also talked about choices, and with it, I mentioned that you have to give your child options so that they can make choices. What do I mean by that? Well choices and options work together to help children's minds grow. It helps them in their creativity, cognitive development and critical thinking skills. How? We use this as a form of redirection a lot in early childhood education, where a child might be falling out, acting crazy, and being upset because of something that they cannot do. This form of calming them down is a form of negotiating. Kinda like good cop bad cop. Gotta choose which cop you gone be on a day to day basis. Give them time to breathe. Give them time to calm down and then after that you give them options. It looks like this. Mary was falling out acting a whole fool because she wanted to stay and play at the carpet, instead of going to use the potty when we were getting ready to go outside. "Okay, Mary, you have two options. You can either sit here with the other teacher while everyone else goes outside and play, or you can go potty so that you can join your class outside. Those are your two options". What am I doing here? I'm giving this child two options. It really doesn't matter to me which one she chooses or not. Right? Somewhat, it kind of does matter. I want her to come outside and play with the children. I'm hoping that she will say okay. I'm hoping she says she wants to go use the potty so she can come outside and get all her playtime. But even if she does not say that, I am not going to be upset. You want to know why? Because she has to learn that there are consequences and repercussions to her actions and to her choices. Say for instance, she did not choose to go potty. Well, that was her choice. Because she did not go potty, she did not get to go outside when her friends went outside. Her time outside was shorter and she might get upset, but that was her choice to make and her lesson to learn.

That is how you give options to redirect behavior. Now Mary knows that every time we go outside and we potty first, if she doesn't potty, she won't get to go outside with her friends right away. The time taken away from her outside time is because of a choice she made. That is what giving your child options does. You could do this for many things.

You could do this for anything. Like dinner time. The child doesn't want to eat their food, but they want more cookies, or they want dessert. They want to eat snacks all day. Instead of giving them a snack, you give them options. Because we all know children don't like eating their food and you say, "Hey, if you eat all your macaroni cheese, and eat all your broccoli, and some of your chicken then you could get dessert when you finish". Make sure you are giving them options in which you don't care whether or not they pick option A, B, C or D. It can be as many options as you want, but it's their choice to choose. Typically what starts to happen after you give children options, children get the thinking. They want to make the choice that they think benefits them the most. If you do this enough you will begin to see it. It's actually quite funny to be honest. Because now you see how their little brains and their minds are working and it's beautiful. So the child would start to think and then they would start to negotiate with you. They will start to change the dynamics of those options by saying things like, "well how about I eat all of my chicken and broccoli? Because I don't really like mac and cheese. And what if I take two bites? Can I still get a snack?" Now you're able to have a conversation that is a real compromise. A real negotiation is going on because now they're conversing back and forth with you. They are trying to see how much or how far you would go, or how far they could take this. Am I right? How far can they push, before you say "oh, no, no deal". This all starts with giving options, and you can do this with children of all ages. It works. Trust me. I do it all the time. So remember, choices and options work hand in hand, and those are just some examples of how to give options. It's a great way to help your child start the decision-making process. To see what they comprehend and to get those critical thinking skills going. It is a great thing to watch unfold. I promise.

Observe. This is my absolute favorite. As you noticed, you probably already heard me mention observe or observation 50 million times in this book. I preach it with anything in regards to teaching, because it is important and very key. The reason it is so important is because without it, you have nothing. When receiving my degree in child development, this is the first thing we had to do to get a better understanding of the children. How they act, what changed their moods, what they like, what they didn't like, I mean, everything. We had to observe, and we also had to write those key details down, especially when it came to enhancing the curriculum we had to put together. Because back then, we had to make up our own curriculum from scratch. And that folks is why creative curriculum is my favorite. The key thing that had to happen or had to be done was observation. Because it shows you what needs to be in your curriculum. If you pay attention, observation shows you what needs to be changed to accommodate another student. Observation also tells you when something is wrong. It shows and tells you if a child isn't receiving the message. It even shows if they are curious or lack confidence, and more. It just showed you everything. So when it comes to curriculum, it is very important. Observation helps you shape your curriculum to cater to those students. Because again, everyone does not learn the same and you cannot teach the same way to every student. Don't ever think they're going to get everything the same way. Understand it the same way. Receive it in the same way or be adaptable to that lesson the same way. That's not always the case. Now, you may have a lot of children that may have similar ways of learning, but that does not mean that they all are going to learn at the same pace.

Observation also tells you when something is wrong such as if a child is sick, or not acting normal. See, when you build relationships with your students, you get to know them. What makes them happy, what makes them sad, what gets them excited. Because you are spending all of this time with these children, when they become sad, you know it. Especially when they become sick, or if something is troubling them deeper. You will know it because you have done all the things we had talked about before in this book. Plus, the most important thing you have done is observe. I encourage everyone to take time out to observe everything. Your work or place of employment, your friends, family members, neighborhood, everything. You don't have to say anything. If you do it right half the time they won't even know you are watching. Observation shows you a lot and tells you how to move and shake. You see I'm from Chicago, and it is almost a habit to be on the lookout. Ironically, I don't like people watching me. Funny right? Buuutttt due to my parents sending me to Mississippi every summer for my entire life, I got over it a little quicker. Because down south bae bay! That's all they do is watch you! If you sneeze different, they would know.

Growing up I've always lived in not so great neighborhoods. Have worked in not so great neighborhoods. Hell, I'm from the hood, ok? ("Now I ain't saying we was from the projects, but every time I wanna layaway or deposit, my dad'll say when you see clothes close your eyelids" haha. Y'all gotta know who that is! Y'all hate loving him haha!) For the most part to me, all the south side of Chicago is considered "ghetto" if you ask me. The closest neighborhood I worked at that was decent in high school was the Ford City area and I had to take a bus through all the hoods to get there. I mean, I got hella stories about that 79th Street bus, you feel me? Long story short, due to my living situation, I got accustomed to observing things way before college. Way before I had no choice but to do so, for classes. Hey, I had no choice but to observe my surroundings before I got to college because I had to ensure my own safety. Going to high school on a bus and working jobs that were completely ways away from my house. Having to travel by bus, for me, observation was a survival tactic. I started working at the age of 16, and many times I wouldn't get home until midnight or 1 am, depending on how that damn bus ran. Observation helped me keep out of trouble and let me know when trouble was coming. It also let me know when people were in trouble as well. I want y'all to think about that for your children and students. Have a proactive, reactive and active mindset when it comes to this observation. Because it could very well save not only your life but your child's life. Now, you know I can't talk about observing without giving you a story. It's my favorite. Therefore because of that, I'm only going to give you just two. Two stories that I think are very key and powerful.

First example. I was working at a school in a toddler class. One of my students, who had a vibrant personality, was not being vibrant. Well, typically when children are sick and parents have to work, if the parents feel something is off, they will give their child some Motrin or Tylenol before bringing them to school, to get the temp down. And that's exactly what was going on in this case. So for two days, I was in constant communication with the parents because I believe in healthy relationships with my parents. I kept asking "are you sure your child is okay? Are they feeling better? Anything new?" And they were like "we went to the doctor." I didn't believe they did, but I'm like okaaaaay. As a teacher, sometimes you can tell when the parents are not being completely honest because they can't afford to keep their child home from school. But because of our relationship, I could properly communicate with them. I knew they had jobs and they were trying. So I just let it slide. Now, the first few days the child is not being vibrant, but still walking at least trying to participate. By the third day the child came in class and just laid down all day. Didn't eat, nor drink. Now, what got me is the child would just lay but wouldn't sleep. They moved around and tossed and turn on the floor, sometimes staring out into a distance, and sometimes grabbing their stomach. Then out of nowhere start to cry, and then stop with no one soothing them. So because we had 12 other toddlers in the class, my first thing was to naturally cater to that child when I could. But most importantly, I stayed observing them. When it came to nap time, the child would do the same thing. So after getting all of the other children asleep, I just held that child. I spoke to the child. They wouldn't respond to me. Their eyes were open. They were breathing. But something was off. I could tell my arms were a safe place yet something was wrong. They still didn't want to eat or drink and move in my arms a lot. No temperature surprisingly. And because they were a toddler, they couldn't verbalize what was wrong. Before nap time was over, I called their parents and told them I was worried. They needed to come pick their child up and take them to the hospital, because what I was observing was far from normal. It was starting to scare me because the child never acted like that. Not even when they're just regularly sick. I said it could be something else going on with the child beyond what we could see. I told them, I'm no doctor, but I do have sickle cell. I explained what the child was showing me, reminded me of how it may look when I would sometimes be in pain internally. I asked if they knew if the child had sickle cell? They said they didn't know, and we just kind of talked a little bit. I ended the conversation by saying, "I know you have to work and I know this may seem normal but it's not. I would hate for something detrimental to happen to your child because I didn't act on my instinct." I told them that they had to take their child to the hospital, and to come and pick up their child now. "Take them to the hospital immediately, and do not bring your child back to school until you have a doctor's note". Now because the child didn't have a temperature, nor diarrhea, or any communicable diseases, technically I couldn't say that. But I was ready to stand behind what I was saying, because I felt so strongly about the child's behavior not being normal. I was truly scared and concerned, so they came right away. It was because of the relationship built with the parents they believed me and considered my words. They knew I truly wouldn't tell them otherwise if I didn't think so. They came and took the child to the hospital right away. The next day they called the school. They wanted to talk to Ms. Johnson. I went to the phone and was welcomed with a warm thank you. They thanked me for making them go to the hospital. They were at the hospital and they wanted to tell me that their child would be out for a couple of days because the child had appendicitis. They said they were going to keep me updated, but they just wanted to thank me. I was just so grateful that we caught it in time, because it would have broken my heart if something happened to that child, especially on my watch.

That's the first example. The next example is a lot harder for me to speak on. Because it did break my heart. At this time, I wasn't a teacher anymore. At that same center I got promoted to assistant director position without the title. Of course, they call me the program coordinator instead, which was fine. Whatever. I wasn't there for titles, I was there for experience and to learn and grow. But they shol' gave me alllll that work though. Hahaha. Moving right along. Well, the first week of training I was doing observations in a kindergarten classroom, because I had to incorporate some changes, when the director pulled me out of the class to show me what was found or observed of one of my former students in my prior class. I go into the classroom and they have the child on the changing table. Everyone has a very somber look on their face, and my mood instantly changes to "what the hell is going on". So I walk up to the table. Say hi to the student. The student is staring off into space, doesn't respond, but then suddenly looks at me. They take off the diaper and show me the student private area which is super open. I instantly asked who dropped the child off because at this point we knew the parent was in hospital for some things that I'm not gonna explain for the sake of privacy. I wanted to know, my eyes instantly welled up with tears that I had to hold back because well, I have a job to do, plus it's other children there. So, naturally, it's a process and we have to go through, call DHS, police, the whole nine. The child also has to go to the rape center, but we have to wait on the ambulance. This whole process has to go on between myself, the director and the student's teachers. We all had to answer some questions for investigation purposes. Then we also had to answer some questions from the state.

While they were talking to the director, I was in the classroom asking the teachers questions. "How was the child acting when they got dropped off?" I asked, because now I have the child and the child wants nobody else. They say the child wasn't acting like their normal self. The child didn't want nobody to really touch them. They stared off into the distance, wasn't talking or playing. (Y'all this child loves to play). I asked "why y'all just now catching this?", because it was later in the morning. Not the afternoon just yet, but to me, close enough. One of the teachers said it was because the child was dry earlier and they didn't change the diaper. So now I'm extremely pissed. I'm thinking, you mean to tell me we could have caught this earlier, if you would have just opened the diaper!? We could have possibly gotten the person who dropped the kids off?! Everyone's emotions were high and the co-teacher calmed me down. She tells me the child was still dry when she changed them too, which she felt was weird so she was giving a fresh diaper anyway and that's when she saw it. So right there on the spot I tell them "from now on, whether the child is dry or not open the diapers". I was so angry. I lay the child on the cot. I sat down for a second. I put my head in my hands and let a few tears fall and wipe my eyes. Then I went to the child sibling's class and asked the teacher if the child had been acting weird or showed any signs of abuse. Now the teachers are looking at me like what the hell is going on? Both teachers in that class were trustworthy and since they had that child sibling in the class I briefly explained what was going on. Told them to not say anything to anyone else in the center and to check the sibling. They did and let me know that there were no signs of abuse for that child. Thank God! By the time the police were done investigating everyone, and the state one by one, the ambulance had arrived to take the child to the rape center. They had finally reached the parent on the phone to let them know what was going on by that time as well. The director comes to me and says I have the parent on the phone and all they keep saying is "tell Ms. Johnson I want her to go with my baby. Ask her to please go with my baby. I want her there". I say "yes, of course! I was gonna ask if I could go anyway". So the director said she was going to go too and to ride with her, she'll take me. Everything inside me that whole day wanted to just cry and kill. The center was located dead smack in the middle of the hood. You better believe one of the teachers that was in that class was from that area too. Before leaving I discreetly say "if you find out who did this make sure you let me know please. Let me know if it gets handled". She say "I got you Mimi". (I know y'all like you the boss, this is how you were talking to your staff, was and did, and sometimes still do, I may have been the boss, but she was my elder. It was mutual respect. Even in my position I still learned from her. I love that lady too). Now if you from where I'm from you know what I'm getting at. I was so angry that if I knew who did it I probably would have tried to handle it myself.

This happened on a Friday. The child was turning 2 on Monday. It's hard. It's so hard for me to even write this without tears in my eyes. Every time I think about it I get mad. This is a situation that they try their best to prepare you for in school, but it's nothing like it, until you are actually handling the situation. We arrive at the rape center and some of the child's other relatives are there. The child comes to me as soon as they see me and the relatives say "you must be Ms. Johnson". I say yes and give everyone a hug and introduce myself. The director introduces herself and then goes to take a phone call. The relatives want to know what happened. I tell them because obviously they know rape is involved. We are at the rape center. We grow silent and you hear sniffles so I say, "I know I'm probably not supposed to do this, but are y'all spiritual, can I pray with you?" And they say yes of course. I say a prayer and you could tell I'm holding back tears. I finished the prayer, and hugged the child, because at that moment I felt like that was the only thing I could do to keep it together. When the people were ready for the child, they were looking for Ms. Johnson. I said I was there and they said the parent requested me to come to the back with the child if they didn't make it in time. I said okay. They said they will be ready in a few. Right before we get ready to go to the back the parent arrives. Crying in total distress, understandably, so I didn't have to go to the back. I tried to calm them down saying that the child needed their strength at this moment. The parent calmed down and went to the back with their child.

One of the family members up front said something to me that I didn't expect, but needed to hear. They told me thank you and they could tell that the child and the parent loved and trusted me a lot. I said thanks in return and I said with a shaky voice "I just wish we could have caught it sooner and grabbed the person at drop off." The lady said "at least you caught it." She proceeded to say "I'm grateful the child came to school today. Because if not, who knows if this would have gotten caught. The child could still be at the same place. Having this done to them. The parent left them with a friend while in the hospital. We know who the friend is and that's all we need to know. It will get handled from here. There is no telling what would have happened if the child didn't come to school. Today is Friday. Y'all closed on the weekend. It could have been Monday when we found out, we don't know. All that matters is, we do now. Thank you for doing your job and loving them above and beyond. Because it's eight o'clock at night. You didn't have to be here but you are". I can't remember the lady name. But I would never forget her words. Once the parent came out, I was able to check on them and what was said about the baby. The parent thanked me. I made sure the parent was going to be okay. After that, the director had to drive me back to my car so I could drive home. I didn't get home till close to midnight. When I arrived home, all I could do was cry. I can only imagine how that parent felt.

See all the questions I had asked the previous teacher before we even talked to the state were questions of observation, in which ironically, were the same questions they ended up asking us anyway, along with some others. Also parents, there are reasons why we have to follow rules, regulations and protocols for childcare centers. Espccially that signing in and signing out! If it wasn't for that sign in and out sheet, the center would have been in huge trouble because we definitely wouldn't be able to say who dropped the child off. I wanted to share this story because it gives a little umph to how important observation is and why it's key. Observation not only helps with teaching and curriculum needs, but everyday life needs as well. Especially when it comes to our children. If you pay attention enough, you will be aware of some of the things you could prevent before it happens. Sometimes observation may help you catch something that people may overlook. And unfortunately, because sometimes the world isn't perfect, through observation you will know how to just simply be there. Whether it is you saying a prayer or sitting in silence, or being a shoulder to lean on or an ear to listen to. Observation will always help you tell what is needed and how to handle a situation a little differently or better. I just feel like we don't use it enough. We don't do it enough. Observation will always be the most important thing that you could do for your child. You don't necessarily have to get involved to observe, you just have to watch. They don't have to know you are watching but you have to watch. I urge everyone to observe their child's interactions! The way they speak, the way they talk, the way they look, how they respond to things, observe it all! It will tell you what to do next. If you don't observe you might miss some key things.

Chapter P

P *is for*
Participate, Peer-to-Peer Learning & Patience

P is for participate, peer-to-peer learning, and patience. Let's start with patience. Boy oh boy. Parents, you can be so impatient sometimes. I'm not going to just say parents, because there are some teachers out there who lack patience too! I don't know why you're a teacher if you're impatient, but hey, you made it through somehow right? With our children, we have to have patience. We have to remember that they don't know nor do they understand the kind of things that we do. So once you understand this, when you are teaching them something, especially something new, you should not get upset. Be patient. Take your time. Do not yell. Do not argue. Do not fuss. Do not fight. Do not huff and puff. Because when you do this, you distract the child. You make them nervous. You could tear away their confidence and make them shut down and now they're not even willing to try. You have to stay cool, calm and collected even when you're upset. Even in moments, especially with our young children, where you have taught them and you know they know. Yet they get to acting like they don't. Like they just didn't do this the other day. Still be patient with them. Because for the most part, they might just be trying you and are probably waiting for you to get upset. You get upset and be like "oh, I don't want to do this now". Then you have given that child exactly what it is that they want. Which is to stop anyway. Let's not do that. Let's not give in to that type of pressure. Let's take a chill pill man. Step back. Calm down and encourage them to try again. Encourage them to start over. It is that simple. Having patience with children while learning is very critical to their learning. If you are impatient with them, they will never learn. You do know that right? Because why? Because you will end up doing things for them. You will start speaking for them. You will start thinking for them. You will not give them the opportunity to learn and grow. You start to hinder your child or your student by being impatient. So remember that the next time you are so annoyed by something you think your child should understand. A lot of times the reason they are taking so long to figure it out is because they don't understand it. Now, you have to refocus your energy back on yourself. What am I (the teacher) doing wrong? Or how could I teach this better? What can I do better to help my student or child understand? Okay, let me rethink this. Let me go back, recalculate, refigure some things out and then try again. When you are teaching, your patience controls the tempo of learning. That is what patience does. Make sure you are controlling the tempo of your child's learning. Controlling the tempo is easier when you participate.

Participate, participate, participate I don't know how else to explain this to you. When your child is learning something new, just like we talked about in chapter 1 with interaction, you have to participate. A lot of times when I am teaching my students we switch roles so that I can participate in the activity. They then become the teacher and I become the student. That is how we build a relationship and that is also one of the ways I learn something new. You could see what they have learned or even mannerisms they may have picked up from you. It's so amazing. It really is.

Have you ever sat down and shown your child how to do a math problem? Did all this work explaining addition and subtraction, then gave them a word problem verbally, having them figure it out without paper and pencil, but only with their mind. Then said, "hey let's switch, you give me a word problem". Now, they're thinking. Look at how they think! It's a reflection of you or your teachings. To challenge my students more, I always use the word trick. Because of that, when we switch roles they are always looking for a way to "trick" me. I always say things like, "Oh, I'm gonna trick you. I'm going to get you this time". That's my way of challenging them to the next level of trying or doing something harder, without them even realizing what they are doing. It's an instant confidence booster as well. Because why? Because they feel like, "you can't trick me!" It motivates them to figure it out. Now what naturally happens because I am that type of teacher to them, when the roles reverse, they try to be that type of teacher to me. And guess what happens? They sit there and they think and they think and they think and they think of a good way in which they could trick me. Through that part of the process, I get to see how they are learning with what it is that I am teaching them. Do you understand how powerful that is? Do you understand what I'm saying? Do you truly get that? As I become a participant, I get to actually see what it is that they are learning from me. Whether its mannerisms, attitude, thought processes, or energy, it's amazing. Then if they mess up, even though I'm still a participant, I can correct and still guide them in the direction in which I knew they were trying to go. Powerful.

Participate while sitting back and watching the children work in everything they do. Observe what it is you have taught them. Let your participation show you where you are going right and where you're going wrong. Let your participation show you your child's mind. So if there is anything to change, now you get to figure it out and fix it along the way. Very, very powerful. Do you understand? So I encourage you to participate in activities with your children. Reverse those roles!

The last P is peer-to-peer learning. This is where social development comes into play, along with emotional development. It tends to be more social because you typically won't see the difference in your child's learning behaviors if they are not around other children. Therefore, I like to encourage parents to have playdates. Put their child into school at an early age of course, or at least put them around other children so that you can observe your child's interactions with other children. It's beautiful. The earlier you do this, the quicker you can find out how your child learns best from peers. (Now this is my theory from experience and what I have seen over the years) From my years of experience working with younger children, I could usually tell when a child learns better from their peers or is motivated better by their peers to learn and engage. I often have to tell my parents that sometimes peer to peer learning could be a good thing or it could be a bad thing. Because for children, it can become a monkey see, monkey do ordeal, right? The bonding that takes place from this with you and your child will take place in those discussions. Constantly be on your child about being a leader and not following people all the time. Let them know, knowing when and when not to follow is super de duper important. Teach them the difference between leading and following. It is important because if they are naturally a peer-to-peer learner, which means they learn more from interacting with their peers more so than they do from anybody else, sometimes it can lead them into trouble. We don't want our children to constantly get in trouble. Having those conversations with your children will be very important.

I know some of you guys are asking how do I know if my child is a peer-to-peer learner? This might be difficult for some people to understand, but I'm gonna try to explain it the best that I can. With a story haha. Alright, I'm gonna use my nephew for example. I knew he was going to be a person who learned from his peers more or faster than he learned from adults. I share this story all the time because he was the youngest I had ever seen this be shown to me through. The children are usually older when I notice. I found out when he was learning to walk. I know. It may sound crazy. But it's true. So my sister and my nephew were living with me for a brief moment. Because he was not in school yet, I set a routine every time I came home. We worked on the alphabet, shapes, colors, finger play, and whatever I could at home with his learning. He was definitely a hands-on learner. If I put something on a TV about shapes and numbers and stuff, it kept his interest momentarily, but then he would fall asleep in my arms or in my bed. I mean every time! No matter the show. But when I came in and I did flashcards and I did colors and things that he could tangibly touch, baby we were rocking and rolling. He would be willing to do that all day! I said okay, I know what type of learner he is. From there I set up a routine where every time I came home from work, me and him would do some type of activity together, and it was so funny. When I came through that door, he was crawling, racing to me like "what we doing today huh huh, what we doing today!" I'm like "hol' up nephew, take a chill pill, let me get out these clothes". He was crawling to me, crawling to my room, opening my door like hurry up! Hahaha it was the cutest thing. I told him "Me and Jay done got you right with helping you learn to crawl on this floor now you just everywhere! Ha!" He would just look at me and wait for the activity and I'm like, "impatient much hahaha". (Yesssss I talk to my babies like this hahaha) So we would do our activities, sing our songs, play with flashcards and things of that nature. I would try to get him to repeat words by saying them, he was getting ready to turn one, so I wanted him to be a little verbal.

He got to the point where he started pulling up on things and trying to take steps but he was scared. So, every day I came home I ended up incorporating that into our routine. I would help him up and help him walk. But he was holding my hands and I wanted him to let go because I knew that he could do it. He was just unsure of himself. I mean, we did this for like two or three weeks. Then one day I took my sister and her child over to my friend's house who had a daughter the same age as my nephew. Before this, he had no other interaction with children his age that I can remember. By this time my friend's child was already walking. They were playing with each other on the floor and a lot of it involved crawling, but bae bae!!! When that little girl jumped up and started walking and ran across the room it was so funny!!! I'm observing their interactions with each other the whole time they are playing, cause I was just excited to see my nephew play with another child. The next thing I see is my nephew give her this look like, "yo' how you do that?" He stands up and then he reaches out for her. She moves away and he starts to walk a little bit but falls. This is the crazy thing, he kept getting up and his eyes were focused on her as he kept looking at her legs. I felt like he was saying in his mind, "shoeeee, she the same height as me, she the same age as me, she was just crawling like me a few minutes ago.... How she doing that?! If she can walk, I can walk! Let me watch how she moving them legs, look she's doing what my auntie and mama be making me practice at home…" hahahaha! The whole time, I mean, EVERY single time she got up to walk, he was like, "let me try! She getting around a lot faster than me!" And right there in that moment, I told my sister, I said, "your son's learning style is peer-to-peer learning and hands-on learning." And she was like, "What do you mean? How do you know that?" I'm like "I'm watching him learn right now". I said "look". She was like, "they playing what you mean"? She was paying no attention or at least didn't know what to pay attention to. I'm paying attention to everything and I just thought it was so amazing. I tell her to watch what her son does every time my friend's daughter gets up and walks.

After we finish for the day and go back home guess what happens. That's right! Sure enough, when we get back home, now my baby is pulling up on stuff and trying to practice walking without me hahaha! Then when I practice walking with him, he became a lot more confident. I feel like he had that image of his friend in his head and he was like "I can do it!" Guess what, two days later y'all he started walking, toddling along with confidence. It wasn't, fall down and then I'm gonna start crawling again, it was I'm falling down but I'm gonna get back up. I'm going to work these legs out. It was amazing to see. Until this day, he still follows his peers a little too much for comfort. My sister started to see what I was talking about a few years ago as well. His learning environment matters a lot! My sister has to have those conversations about being a leader and not a follower with him. My sister now sees the difference. He had the opportunity to be in two different learning environments while in school, and she was able to visually see and experience the difference. One was a more positive and structured learning environment, yet hands-on. He was soaring and taking off. But when he had to go to another environment that was a little bit chaotic, not negative, just lacking structure, he mirrored the environment. I know you may be thinking, well that's with all children. NO! Some children you can put into a chaotic classroom and they won't become a monkey see monkey doer. They'll be looking at yo' children, like these mugs crazy. They are not easily influenced, pressured, or phased by their peers. Don't get it twisted either, peer to peer learning can be useful and good. Hey, from observing his peers while playing outside, my nephew also taught HIMSELF how to ride a bike without training wheels. HA! He skipped that whole process and went straight to 2 wheels, at the age of 4, just by watching his peers. That's talent. Y'all know that some of these babies out here are 3 and 4 years old, and can't push the pedals on a tricycle? Can't balance on much of anything, let alone a bike. I'm super proud of him. I just continue to encourage my sister to be careful with who she chooses to put around him because that is how he learns best through his peers. You know, so you have to be careful with that.

Now another example that I'll give you, so it won't seem so biased hahahaha is an example of a three-year old that I had in my class. This three-year-old was almost the youngest but was not the youngest. This example happens a lot with a lot of my three-year-olds to be honest. I have a lot of three-year-olds who see other children in class succeeding in doing things differently than them, it looks very interesting, and they want to do it too. That's fine, but they may not be on the same level as the other students. They may be tremendously below. But when they want to participate in these different activities, I don't discourage them, I have conversations with them. I say, "Hey, this child knows how to recognize all their letters. They know what all of them sound like, so now this child is capable of starting the process I am doing with them. You are not there yet and you have to work a little bit harder to get there. I need you to focus and pay attention and do all of the things I mentioned before we get you there".

Although some people are upset about inclusion, I understand the benefits. Do I like putting children into categories like we used to do back in the day with gifted, regulars, and honors? Yeah, I'm for that too. Either way, it doesn't matter to me because I am an excellent teacher. I'm going to figure it out. With that, I understand the difficulties in inclusion. Yet, I also understand the positivity of an inclusive classroom setting as well. As early childhood educators, we have no choice but to follow the inclusive model whether we want to or not. None of our children are ever on the same level coming in. We are always required to practice inclusion 24/7 365. I guess that's why the model doesn't bother me. I can see the benefits of it being separated into those categories in elementary school, and high school though, more than having the inclusive classroom. Anyway, with that being said, what happens is the children see the other children being able to do different activities in which they want to be involved. This in return motivates them to try a little harder and be a little better. It simply happens that my students end up all becoming very good leaders because that's what I promote in my class. That's if me and the parents are on the same page, because I do have parents who just don't want their children to be involved in anything. Which doesn't make any sense to me, but hey, whatever floats your boat.

In this example, this child could not read and saw other children working on sight word books. That child wanted to do it. But I had to tell the child " I need you to learn your ABCs. First uppercase, lowercase, and then sounds before we could start working on sight words". That's all that child needed to know. When that child saw everybody else doing it, the child started to focus a lot more. And bam! That child was on their level. Now if I do work with a child, not in a group setting and that child does not see what other children are doing, that child can not gauge the other children's success. The child has nothing to compare themselves to and is a little less motivated. I know when I say compare, it may sound negative, but in this magnitude, it's really not. You know how in entrepreneurship we're always saying, well, you have to surround yourself with others who are doing what you want to do. Who are being and living in those moments in which you want to live and be in. It is the same thing. It's not necessarily a comparison, as much as it is being able to see somebody capable of doing the things that you are yet to be able to do. Which gives you a little bit of motivation. Because it says, well, if they could do it, I could do it too. It makes you want to be around those people a lot more because you know that eventually, your time is coming. Right? You're going to get there. So it's the same thing with education. We're not gonna turn motivation into a negative thing for children. We are all subconsciously comparing a little. But a great learner learns to take what they see from others and apply it for and to themselves as well. A child can't necessarily grasp or concede to the idea of something that they haven't first been introduced to. Therefore, let's look at it like that. Let's look at peer-to-peer learning as a notion of children being influenced by other children that they may look up to, who can introduce them to a concept that they may not completely understand when receiving the lesson from an adult. They are receiving it from other children that they are encouraged by. More importantly, those children motivate them to want to do better, or become better. I say there's nothing wrong with that. What you have to do is teach your child which apple tree is the wisest to pick from. (For those whose heads that went over, go listen to some Erykah Badu) In other words, teach them how to choose their circles wisely. If it ain't elevating them, uplifting them, or helping them grow, they don't need to be surrounded by it! That's for everyone, but especially my babies who are peer-to-peer learners.

Chapter Q

Q *is for*
Question

Q is for question. Now, you hear me say this a lot along with observe. I get on everybody's nerves because I do this a lot. I could never understand why people get so mad when you ask questions. Yeah, it's power in questioning everything okay? That is the only way we learn. If you have a question to ask, ask it. I now have a new understanding of the saying, there's no such thing as a stupid question. First, I used to be like, yeah it is, and quiet as kept, deep down inside, I still do think that sometimes. Especially when you're not listening, but that's just me being petty, sometimes. You should question things and allow your children to question you as well. And I know…Whew, especially for our community, that is something terrible. "You don't question no adults." "I make the rules here!" You know, that's what we think. That's how we feel, and guess what, you are entitled to your feelings, but how else are children or anybody who's trying to get an understanding of you, supposed to learn? How they gone know what you stand for, what you mean, what you're trying to teach, what you believe in, if they don't question it? And I don't mean question, like call you out cause you lying (unless you're a liar, then I don't know what to say about that, except aren't we too old) But actual questions so that they could gain understanding, whether it is of you, your beliefs, ideology, where you come from, or anything. Yeah, I often tell my parents I work with, that they must question the teachers, the schools, and themselves. What is it you want, or what is it that you want your child to receive? Whether it's from being in that class, from attending that school, or just from being in your presence. You must ask yourself that too. You have to ask yourself important questions. Questioning improves the mind. It improves the thought process, the decision-making process, comprehension, and cognitive development of the brain. When you ask your child questions or allow your child to ask you questions, you get to see how they are thinking and what they may or may not understand. It becomes your opportunity to clarify or to make the process of understanding better. I think as a people we get away from this too much. It's my way or the highway, right? "Don't question me." "What I say goes." When I'm working and I question my bosses or superiors, it's like, I become a threat. I get in trouble. I start being treated differently. It's like, don't have a mind of your own. Don't ask these questions. Don't start digging for answers. Because once you do, it naturally becomes a problem.

I say to people who have an issue with people questioning things, Why? HAHAHAhahaha. What is it that you're trying to hide? What is it that you don't want me to know? Most importantly, what is it that you don't want me to understand or learn? Why don't you want me to ask any questions? That's my concern. Like I said, Yes, I get in trouble with jobs when I start asking questions, and I don't even care. I'll get in trouble. Go ahead, feel intimidated. You can feel angry. You can feel what's the word they like to use for Black women? I'm always an angry, insubordinate, intimidating, condescending, Black woman who's not a team player when I start questioning things. Yes, it pisses me off, because I'm like, hey I'm just here trying to get a clearer understanding of what is going on and how we operate here. Because what is going on is not what my employee handbook says is supposed to be going on. Hahaha. No, but in all seriousness. I ask questions about things that I truly don't understand. Like why is this child who clearly should be in an 8-year-old class in here with the babies? Or why does that teacher have her shoes off, holding this little boy down with her nasty ass feet? I swear yall I be seeing some crazy ish. Let me share this story real quick I was an undergrad doing an internship at this school for the summer in Guthrie OK. Now, this was a white school, weren't many Black people there. This older woman who was in my class getting her Associates degree used to work at this school as the librarian. She was coming back to school so they could pay her more. Had that lady working there all those years not paying her jack diddly squat! Made me mad. Anyway, I used to go help her. I remember doing this dope ass Dr. Suess big gigantic Hop on Pop book with chalk for a Dr. Suess event. I was so proud of myself y'all! It was dope! And do you know that school kept my artwork cause I used their supplies?!? I can't even find the pictures anymore. That was my best artwork ever! Any who, over the summer, I was offered a job with their summer program. I don't understand how it was supposed to run, it made no sense to me, so don't ask. I just went in at certain times, and played in the classroom with the students and played with them on the playground. It was very non-educational. Well during naptime, we had a child who should have been with the 8, 9, and 10 year olds. Those children didn't take naps. During naptime, they watched a movie in the gym room. This child we had was diagnosed with having MR (Mental Retardation). The child could not speak, just made noises. This child was big too and walked around aimlessly all the time. Now I wasn't sure why this child was in the room with the 3, 4, and 5-year-olds. Even with MR, the child could be upstairs fine. They said it was a development thing, but the child was way beyond that of a 3, 4, or 5-year-old. I simply asked, did they try to see what it would be like for the child upstairs with their age group, and they were like no. The babies were scared of this child because the child was huge, and sometimes did hurt the smaller ones. Well during nap time, the child would never go to sleep. Now, this was my first time seeing a child hunch the floor. It was several of them at this school that did it, and naturally, I'm like why are these kids in here masturbating. Y'all I was thinking, "do I need to call the people?" So they explained to me that it was a coping mechanism or something for the children to go to sleep. I'm like "oooookkkaay". Well the child with MR not only hunched the floor, but played with them self as well every naptime while making obscene noises. I was weirded out y'all, like never in my life had I ever experienced anything like this. Now mind you, I'm still in school learning about how to report people and all that. So I didn't know. One day I come to work, and it's during nap time, and this fat teacher had her shoes off and her corolla roast feet, on the MR child's back, pinning the child down to the cot, trying to rock the child to sleep with her feet. I was sooooo mad. I also was the only Black teacher working there, so I didn't say anything the first day. On the second day I came to work and saw the teacher doing it again. (I was extra shocked cause this was a white teacher doing this to a white child. I don't know what I thought. I know, I thought that white people had their ish together, in a more solidarity way. Especially when it came to their children. I would soon learn that they were just as fucked up as everyone else in the world, honestly. Just in a different manner. A lot of them were just "gifted" better opportunities. Remember before college, I had only seen and experienced Black and Hispanic people doing each other wrong, and white people doing us wrong. I had never seen white people doing each other wrong before then, except in the movies). This time I had to ask. I was like "why you got the child pinned down like that?" She says "so the child won't get up." So then I start asking questions like, "why don't I just take the child upstairs and see how the child does up there". She like, "oh no thanks". So I asked another teacher, "that's what yall do, pin children down if they won't go to sleep?" I'm like, "do they have to go to sleep?" Asking all types of questions, because I didn't like what I saw being done to the child, and I did not have that mothers number. Honestly, at that time, I wasn't too sure on how to approach white parents about their children anyway. Just being honest. Sometimes y'all can be a little different and difficult when teachers are trying to sincerely help you. Plus I was a young Black teacher at that. Not saying that any other race of parents aren't difficult either. It's just at that time in my life, I was not fuckin with y'all. It was very different. Longer story short, after those two days of asking questions, I got fired the next week. Ha! The librarian lady who took classes with me, who also got me the job, was so mad at the time. Until I told her what happened and then she went and made a call, and was fine. She told me "fuck em". She said I did the right thing by trying to help the student and speaking up. I told her "if I ever caught someone doing that to my child I would be going to jail". I couldn't understand how they were ok with doing that to a child with special needs.

It happens all the time. That example in chapter C I gave you, happened 6 or 7 years later, and that was a Black school. So the minute I start speaking up for myself, or others and start asking questions, it becomes a problem. I want everyone to know it is ok to question things. Especially things that are morally wrong. Teach your children to question those things. I honestly feel if more people started to question things and speak out against what's wrong, the world would be a better place. What I believe the world is missing is that lack of understanding of one another. Our histories, cultures, and values. How can we truly understand it, when they don't teach accurate history, and feed us lies about one another. See, the only way you will ever know the truth is if you choose to seek it. If you don't know something if you don't UNDERSTAND something, why not seek clarity? People are out here running around making assumptions about things that they don't know about. You would be so surprised what could happen if you open your mouth and ask a question or two. You would be so surprised at the sorts of good conversations that can come from questions. I learn so much about different cultures and backgrounds from asking questions. I gain new perspectives and new levels of appreciation and respect. Why would I want to keep those things from any children when they ask questions? Better yet, why would I do anything to deter them from wanting to ask questions? Because questioning is a part of learning. Accept it as part of the growth process. Stop taking people asking you questions so personally, or in the wrong way. Be happy that I ask you questions. That shows that I care enough about you, your situation, your persona, or your teachings enough to want to understand more. Also, there's power in asking questions. Especially the right questions. Because unfortunately, the world runs on a don't ask don't tell axis. I used to think it was just men, because they do it so effortlessly. But I have learned and grasped that it is in everything that this crazy world does. So don't be afraid to ask questions! Asking questions, especially the right ones, can be valuable. Valuable to your growth, wisdom, and understanding of not only your job, family, or the world but of yourself as well.

Chapter R

R *is for*
Relate, Responsibility, Repetition, Routine & Redirect

R is for relate, responsibility, repetition, routine and redirect. Again, sounds like a lot, but isn't. Let's start with my favorite relate. Now y'all know my motto. You can't teach'em if you can't reach'em. What does that mean? That means if you cannot relate to that child in any way, shape, form, or fashion, then it is going to be a lot harder for you to teach them.

It'll be a lot harder to get through to them in difficult situations, lessons, moments, and conversations. That's why bonding moments are so important. That's why everything talked about from chapter A up until this point has been so important! Even if you don't understand some of the music, thoughts, ideas, shows, or whatever your child loves, creating time to do so through interactions and conversations can give you the opportunity to. I see this problem with a lot of teachers who are of different races. Like for instance, the teachers who are white and working in all Black schools. You don't live in those neighborhoods. You don't watch the same programs that those children watch. You don't speak the same language that those children speak. You probably don't even eat the same food that they eat. It is a completely different atmosphere. You know, some of y'all haven't even gone through any struggles that they can relate to. But you work in these communities and try to boast or flaunt your "power". Not knowing you don't have any, acting the "This is how it's done. Oh, I'm the teacher, you listen to me, what I say goes" way. It really repels students into thinking you don't care for real. Why? Because it comes off as if you are leading with judgment, instead of sincerity. Y'all really be struggling and thinking it's the children's fault, or the parent's fault, you can't teach. No, it's your fault! Most Black teachers are 100 times more relatable to that child and can understand some things that you can't. Knowing that it still shocks me when Black teachers try to work through power and not compassion like most of the white teachers I've seen do it. Now, I'm not saying all Caucasian teachers are like that. I've met some pretty dope white teachers, and even had some. They understood the assignment though, in these all Black schools. Even some of the most boring teachers. They made whatever they were teaching about relatable, or interesting. They did it without trying to speak like us or act like us too. They were totally themselves! Opened up about some of their history with their family and everything. They came to class and did their white girl or white boy dance, and asked the students to teach them some moves. Didn't belittle or look down upon the students' clothes or hair. Nor did they have to try to be like or act like someone they weren't. In fact they asked questions! Tried to understand the culture, without being disrespectful. They started deep and candid conversations and related it, some way, somehow back to the subject at hand. They didn't have to yell, belittle, or say over and over again to the students. "This is MY class", hahaha. Y'all it really be teachers out there struggling to get control of the class. Classroom management is a real skill! Those teachers lack those relatable skills. You are not even gaining the respect of your students because of the way you are being. To make matters worse, you refuse to get to know them. You are missing the opportunity to understand some of the struggles and some of the things that they are going through. Moments like those will help you make better decisions in moments where you are to decide whether to hold them accountable or be understanding. What do I mean by that? I'll use this most common example I have seen at all schools from childcare to elementary.

A child arrives at school late, and misses breakfast by two minutes. Your class is still eating though. No one is nowhere near done eating. The child is clearly hungry, but because he or she missed the cut-off time, you don't allow them to eat. Even though you have hella food sitting right there in their face. Their classmates are eating in their face! Damn, they can't at least get a milk and an orange or something? They just gotta sit there, because they were 2 minutes late? Now the whole entire morning, y'all mad at each other. You are mad at the child because they are being disruptive because they're hangry. The child is mad at you because they're hungry, and because of that they can't concentrate on anything else besides I'm hungry. Also, the fact you sat there and allowed other children to sit and eat in their face because they were two minutes late.

This goes for any teacher no matter the race. If you have not taken the time out to learn your students, you are not going to understand why that child is giving you such a hard time. If you do know and don't care because you feel like, what you're doing is going to make them a better person, or more responsible, it's not. The only thing it will do in those moments is make the child that you refuse to let get a bite of food every time they're a minute late, feel like you ain't never struggled in your life and you don't care. They may actually be trying to get to school on time, just so they can eat. If their parents are dropping them off, they have no control over that. That child may be taking care of their siblings at home and offering them the last of their food. The only time they do get to eat may be when they are at school. And that says a lot cause school lunches are nasty as hell in these neighborhoods unless it's the pizza. But you don't know that, and you won't know if you don't get to know the child. Can you relate? To be honest, whether you can or not, there is always a better way than escalating the problem, to help the child be more "responsible" or "accountable". Ultimately, how would you want someone to treat your hungry child who doesn't have food at home to eat?

Then some of you teachers can't even start the process of getting to know the children, because in all actuality you suck as a teacher. You don't need to be teaching. I'm sorry. People who lack classroom management skills, just come out of teaching until you learn that skill. We all know that the beginning of the school year is where you set the tone for your class. What tone are you setting, on day one? I am to be walked over? I don't care, I'm just here for a check? I can't teach anyway, this is a waste of both our time? I mean what? You can't even grab their attention long enough to have a conversation. Teaching ain't for the weak now. You can't be crying and hollering "these kids", "these kids," "these kids." What ARE YOU DOING?! Ha! They are doing exactly what they are supposed to do, which is to try you. Have energy. Explore. Talk. Chit chat. Question. Challenge, and the list goes on and on. You are supposed to know how to regain that focus and redirect the attention. Lawd! Here's a tip for all my first-time teachers. Week one, use that time to get to know your students. In all aspects. While setting the rules and tone of the class.

I've walked in, been called in, and had to sub too many classrooms where I see teachers walkout in full-blown tears. Tip number two, don't EVER let a classroom full of rowdy children see you cry, ESPECIALLY if you work in the hood. Ain't no coming back from that, them babies know they got you. I'm laughing as I write this because those visions and memories of me being asked to step into classrooms by teachers who never come back are popping up. I'm sitting in the classroom the whole day teaching and just building with the students. Then I realize their teacher ain't came back. I gotta sub the next day or week or two weeks, and I'm in there asking the students what they did to their teacher. Ha! Tip number three for you teachers, games are the best. So if it's a boring reading lesson, make it a fun reading lesson. Throw a game at the end of that joint, and bam! You got class participation, recap, and enjoyment. One of my top go-to's for behavioral issue classes, is finding out what the students like to do in their free time. Ok, you give me my time to teach, you participate, answer questions, learn. Then I give you a certain amount of time to do whatever before we go to the next lesson. As long as ain't nobody acting a fool either. I call it a break. It works.

Relatability is powerful. If children feel like you understand where they come from, their struggles, and some of the things they have going on, they will be more inclined to listen to your advice, your perspective, and your suggestions. But when you can't even take the time out to get to know them or try to relate, you just become another body. Somebody that doesn't care. Remember there are other ways you can be relatable as well. It's not just through struggle. You can relate through music, books, poetry, art, television, the list goes on. There are so many ways in which you could be relatable to a child and use that to reach them so you're able to teach them.

Next Responsibility. Responsibility is a double-edged sword. It's hard to explain this because I want parents to give their children responsibilities, but I don't want them to overdo it. I know in my culture, we come out the womb with responsibilities. I don't care what anybody says, it's like as soon as you start walking, you got a responsibility! It's children taking care of children galore!

We have to balance responsibility. A lot. I want parents to use responsibility as a way to give their children a boost of confidence and to teach them skills for survival they need to learn. Children like helping. They like the feeling of having done or been a part of something that is great. There are great learning moments in responsibilities given. That's why in early childhood education, we give them jobs. Whether it's something as small as setting the table, passing out cups, and spoons, being the line leader, and things of that nature. It gives them a sense of pride in being able to showcase their talents or help out the teacher. We should incorporate these responsibilities at home. It brings a level of accountability to the children because they are required and expected of certain things. This way when they get older, they won't run from responsibilities easily. There's a level of maturity to responsibility as well. Somethings your children just aren't responsible enough to handle, giving responsibilities at a younger age will help with those conversational moments. Especially when those "why can't I" questions start to arise.

It is when your children have so much responsibility that it becomes a concern. Like your 10-year-old watching your four-year-old, your five-year-old and your newborn. They aren't able to be a child themselves, because they are too busy being the part-time parent. That's when responsibility could become a bit too much. Although it does give us strength, and it gives us character, (and I say "us" because I was one of those children), we had to grow up at a young age. It can be overwhelming and super stressful at times. It's a lot to feel like, everyone has to count on you, but you can't really count on others. I had to grow up at the age of nine. My mom got sick and had a brain aneurysm that burst while in surgery, causing her to have a stroke. From that time, my life was never the same. For one, I was an angry child. I was sad. I was hurt. I was scared. The woman who took care of me my whole entire life was no longer able to. I know y'all like, whole entire life, you were 9. Yea well I felt like my life was ending. I had sickle cell and there were a lot of transitions happening. We were moving, my mom was in and out of the hospital. I didn't like the new house, new neighborhood, new school. Then it became an even bigger mess. My mom went back to the old house with my two older siblings and my dad stayed at the new house with me and my younger siblings. It was battles and a whole bunch of stupid ish. All I knew was we were one, then we were split into two. I was no longer the middle child, I became the oldest. Not only that, I had to take care of my younger sisters, but felt I had a responsibility to take care of my mom as well. Because she was the only person I could remember as a child who was with me at the hospital all the time when I got sick. Who helped me at night when I was in pain, who rubbed my back, legs, and arms when they were hurting. Who gave me baths, who cooked me food, who made sure that I was well at all times when I was sick. On top of that, still made sure I stayed on top of my homework at all times no matter how sick I was. I still have the mark on my figure to prove it. I don't remember my dad being there in those moments, you know? He was there, but not like my mama, you know my mom she took care of her baby. It was a lot, she helped me feel better. Making sure I got my medicine, making sure I stayed on top of my schoolwork, making sure I did everything that I was supposed to do regardless of my condition. From birth. Did my dad take over after that? Yes, but that is also when I had to grow the fuck up. I was in charge of doing my sister's hair, and helping them out with their homework. Cooking them food to eat, making sure we got home from school, washing clothes, cleaning dishes, just all types of stuff. It was very frustrating and overwhelming. I got in trouble for a lot of the things they did for being little assholes. I had to damn near take them with me everywhere I went and was responsible for their safety at all times. Did they know this? NO! So it was always a fight. We were close, but in the most dysfunctional ways ever. I can't explain it. That would take another book. Hell, I'm still trying to understand the dynamics of our relationships. Now y'all see why I went so far away to school. Ha! I just wanted to focus on me for once. I didn't want to be responsible for no one else for a while! I am still grateful for those experiences. They have made me an incredibly strong person, with great critical thinking skills. Did I have to overcome past trauma? Yes, as any person going insane should hahaha. Granted, our situation at home was caused by some traumatic experiences and events, especially with my mom getting sick at a young age. But what about the people whose parents are perfectly fine. Parents who are perfectly capable of taking care of the children, but simply just don't want to. They are not working, they are just out in the streets all day and night. Living life as if they don't have any responsibilities and have their children taking care of their babies. See the responsibility the parents run from, is put onto the child, or someone else. All because they want to run the streets. I have to ask parents who do this, did you have any responsibilities when you were younger? Or did you not? Was it a mix? What? I sincerely want to understand.

I feel like this is why a lot of men have a hard time when they come from single-parent homes. Because a lot of the time they had to grow up at a young age. Or felt the need to have some level of responsibility to help out the house, because they see mama struggling. Dad is nowhere around. Now they selling drugs or doing whatever starting at the age of 10 to help pay bills and survive. Whether we like to think so or not, that responsibility is a lot. And a lot of emotions come with that level of responsibility that is usually pent up inside. Although some situations are just unfortunate, and parents are trying to make it, best they can, I want you to stay alert or aware of your children's feelings and mental state.

The whole purpose of this conversation is to say that responsibility is good. I believe everyone should give their child some level of responsibility. I think there are parents out there who don't give their children any level of responsibility and that can be just as detrimental. I believe that we can do a better job of balancing those levels of responsibilities though. We can do a better job of not forcing it on our children. I believe it is handled better by children if they accept the responsibility and all that comes with it. Only when they are ready, willing and want to do it. I believe as our children grow, we should do a better job at looking at how they mature into the position instead of forcing maturity on them. There's levels of responsibility. We want children to understand priorities and accept the responsibility to handle them without it being so harmful to the mind.

Redirect. It works hand in hand with options and choices. I want everyone to remember that, when we are redirecting children, we are rechanneling their attention or focus onto something else. We do this by gaining their attention or distracting them from something that is upsetting them. Whatever it is that gets them riled up, whether negatively or positively, usually leads to fussing, fighting, arguing, or crying. The goal is to either foresee it or while in the midst of it, grab their attention quickly and direct it towards something else. So say, for instance, your child is asking you for some cookies because they just saw some cookies in your hand. Now the attention is on the cookies. You don't give them cookies and they start to cry. So you yell out, "look at Mickey over there dancing!" This may throw them way off, and they stop thinking about that cookie. As long as it's out of sight. While they're looking for Mickey, you better make sure you put those cookies out of sight. Keep them out of sight, and now they are no longer thinking about cookies, they're thinking about Mickey.

Another short example. Two children are fighting over a toy. You want to redirect one of the child's attention to something else. You say, "Hey Aaron is working with the blocks, but wow, look at these magnets over here! Look what I could do with these magnets." Now, the first person who comes over there to the magnets is no longer thinking about the blocks. They get to play with the magnets. You will have moments where both of them might try to run to the magnets. That's when you can give them choices or say something like, "Only one of you can play with the magnets for now. You guys were just arguing over blocks, now only one of you can play with the magnets. You guys can choose to take turns later, or how about you guys switch in 5 minutes?"

Those are moments of redirecting. When you address the situation by putting out the fire before it starts a bigger flame early on. Redirection is one of the biggest things that we do in early childhood education for disciplinary purposes. It is a tool that is used to refocus the children or regain their attention. To point it in another direction so that it causes less drama or issues. I suggest all parents become very familiar and use redirection for their babies because it definitely works. Remember their attention spans are very short. Although that could be a challenge for us as teachers. We could learn to use that to our advantage in moments of chaos or conflict.

I hope by now all of you guys understand that you have to repeat yourself 50 million times a day for children to learn. The younger they are, the more you have to repeat yourself. So in all actuality, it may turn out to be 100 million times a day. If you think that you're gonna have a child in your custody, that you won't have to repeat yourself to 50 million times a day, you, my good friend are in for a rude awakening. Repetition is how children learn. They have to hear it over and over and over and over again. So what is it that they have to hear? Words of encouragement. Instructions. You have to repeat why or how something is wrong and how to make it better. Everything you do. Everything. You have to repeat every single thing. That's why in school, we go over the same thing over and over and over again until they understand it. Then once they understand it, we can move on over to the next thing that we have to repeat 50 million times a day. I know some of y'all got some tireless children that are like the Energizer Bunny! They do a lot. They are the funniest ones and those are the ones that you have to repeat to the most. I'm not gone lie, those babies crack me up because they will stare right at you when they are doing something they know they're not supposed to do. They will look at you while you tell them not to do it and still do it! Ha! They will act like they don't know but they know! Don't let these babies fool you. They definitely know what's up. But they are so cute and cuddly, tiny and small, so precious, you let them get away with murder and that's how they get you. Remember to repeat, repeat, repeat. You have to repeat in words and you have to repeat in actions. That is the only way the child is going to learn. Also, be mindful of what actions you choose to repeat over and over again in front of your child. As much as they learn directly from you, they learn even more indirectly from you as well! Be mindful of what you are showing them.

That brings me to routine. Routines are actions on repeat. Routine can work hand and hand with structure as well. We have routines for everything in life already, you just may not realize it's a routine. It could be a positive routine or a negative routine. It all depends on how it affects you and what you get out of it. When we are getting up for work every day, the manner in which we prepare ourselves for work is the routine. Most of the time you never deviate from the routine unless something has changed in your schedule. The way you get out of bed, take a shower, and get dressed, is a routine. Same thing goes for what you do at night and midday. You do the same things, in the same order, every time, majority of the time. Till this day, routines that my mom embedded in us still sits with me as an adult. I call it the coming home from school routine. Back in the day, we had to wear uniforms for school. I always like to think that I had five sets of clothing types. We had our church clothes, school clothes, outside clothes, our "nice" clothes, and pajamas, my favorite. (Yes y'all I like to be comfortable, pajamas are my favorite type of clothing hahaha. I would wear them everywhere if I could) Well, every time we transitioned from someplace to home we always had to take whatever clothes we had on off, if they were nice, and put on our "outside" clothes. So the school routine consisted of once we got home from school, taking off our uniform to put on our outside clothes, but we couldn't go outside until our homework was done. We were required to sit at the table, and do our homework. You could not move from the table until mama checked your homework. Once your homework was done you could then go outside. Depending on the time of day and how close it was to dinner time, we could either go on the porch, or we had to stay on the block. The house door stayed open, the screen door closed, but don't be running in and out the house! That's how you end up having to stay inside the house. Depending on how my mama felt, when we came in for dinner, we had to stay in or were allowed back out, but had to be in by the time the street lights came on. After we ate, we washed up, put on our pajamas, and went to bed. This was a routine my mom had us do, that I still remember vividly, and I still kinda do to this day as an adult. Like, I come home, take off my work clothes, wash up, because I'm working with babies, and I put on my "play" clothes. Depending on what I'm not doing, those are my pajamas hahaha. I also refuse to sit on my bed or let anyone get into or sit on my bed with their outside clothes. Ha! For some reason, that routine with my mom stuck with me the most, outside of Sundays are clean-up days. Throw some dusties on the radio and get the cleaning! Think about some of the routines you have embedded into your life that stem from your childhood. Now ask yourself what routines are you creating for yourself and your family? A good routine is needed and will make an ever-lasting impression. Know that you are creating them whether you know it or not. For example, if you are not with the mother anymore, and you tell your children you are going to come and get them every weekend, but you don't. You have now created a routine of letting your children down, and not being a man of your word. Now not only does this cause the children not to believe in anything you say.

You have indirectly caused a lifelong memory of routine letdowns. Is that the routine you want to be most known for?

Routines and structure are beneficial for our everyday life. Regardless if you realize it or not, your entire life is a routine, from the time you are born. You have a sleep schedule. You have a poop schedule. You have an eating schedule. Then you have a work routine and schedule. You have a time when you get up. You have a time to arrive at work. You have a designated routine for work. Everything is a form of routine. It's when those routines lack structure, that it can start to become a headache not only for the children but ourselves as well. Children can have a routine of chaos if structure isn't implemented. This leads me to our next letter.

Chapter S

S *is for*
Structure, Self-Awareness, Standard & Social Development

    Children definitely need structure. Structure is an arrangement or plan. It has a relation to the routine in some way, form, or fashion. If you don't have structure with the routine, you usually have chaos. The children are doing whatever the hell they want, whenever they want, and however they want to do it. If you do not want chaos you have to have structure. Put it into place. That's one of the biggest reasons why I choose not to work at play-based centers. I know you are wondering, aren't all child care centers play-based? Yes, in some form, because children learn through play. But there are some centers where that's all they do the entire 12-hour day. It is student-guided, instead of teacher-guided. So, to me, it feels as if you are just babysitting and watching them play all day long!! Ohhh how boringgggggg! It makes the day go by entirely too slow. Centers like those are what we like to call play-based centers. A curriculum-based center has a curriculum. They have moments and times throughout the day where learning is teacher-guided, and then moments where learning is student-guided. It's a healthy balance. Those are the centers I choose to be a part of because they are more structured. It has more of a routine and a plan in place. In fact, the teacher is heavily involved in the lesson planning and scheduling process. Unless the school has a curriculum that the teachers have to abide by. Then the teachers become partially involved in the planning process, because most of the work, or lesson planning is done for them. Which I'm ok with unless you are a "by the book" teacher. That's what I call teachers who can't derive from the lesson plan to diversify the student's ability to learn. When all teachers have to do is get the materials together and teach, it becomes a challenge for them to think of creative ways to make the lesson better. Especially when their students are not being challenged and are bored at school, causing behavior issues to arise. Any who.

Working at centers where the children could do whatever they want whenever drives me nuts! I need structure. I need a routine. I need a plan of direction. I feel as though it is critically important for children, especially young ones to have that as well. It keeps them focused, aware, and most importantly safe. Structure is also a form of discipline. It not only keeps students, but us as adults, aligned with the task at hand as well. We get discombobulated when we have too much going on at one time with no plan of action or structure. Can you imagine what the world would look like if it looked like a toddler classroom with no routine or structure?! Ha! Or any age group, classroom with no routine or structure? My cousin and I have talks about this all the time. I said it would look like episodes of The Walking Dead. My cousin said it'll be worse. It'll look like a real-life version of The Purge. I must say tho', those classrooms with teachers who don't know how to manage the class, dooooo be looking purgerous! Hahahaha! They be like "OFF WITH THE TEACHER HEAD!" Ha! I know some of you teachers reading this may think what I said was not funny…and I am here to tell you… IT ISSSSS!!! HA! If you're mad, you are probably that teacher that needs to implement structure in your classroom or home! We have this saying amongst teachers, we can imagine what your house looks like by the way your classroom looks. The organization or lack thereof tells it all. If you are wondering why no one wants to eat the food you bring to the potluck from home, that's why buddy! Not to mention, we probably also saw the many times you were supposed to wash your hands and DIDN'T. Little nasty! And don't tell me you got pets at home, and I see you not wash your hands and your classroom is a mess! HA! Don't you dare ask me to try something you made! Hahaha! My answer is always going to be I can't eat that, it's against my religion! Hahahaha! SORRY SOMEBODY HAD TO SAY IT! Ha! We ALL be thinking it! Whispering in the teacher lounge, "who cooked that, who brought that". Ok ok, stick a fork in me I'm done!

To sum this all up, structure is important! As you can see, it works hand and hand with routine. I'm going to throw organization in there as something it works hand and hand with as well. I challenge everyone reading this to get some structure in your life if you don't have it. For those of you who do, what does the structure in your home or classroom say about you? Do you have hella food that you have to bring back home or get rid of after the potluck?

That was a great lead right into my next topic for S. Self Awareness. This one is another difficult one. Because a lot of adults aren't self-aware. They don't even know themselves. So how would they even be able to teach it to their children? People can't even be honest with themselves, so how do we expect them to be honest with each other? At the beginning of this book, I said, I want you to do a SWOT analysis of yourself. That was a form of self-awareness. Have you been doing it throughout the book? Where can you be better? Where can you be stronger? What opportunities presented themselves to you? Do you see yourself as a threat in some areas? It's important that you know this about yourself. You see, one thing's for sure about children, they are some of the most honest creatures you'll ever meet. But somewhere along the lines, they begin to lose that honesty, purity, and innocence. The question is why? Well, I like to think it's because society is so messed up! We inadvertently mess up our children. They no longer become aware of their feelings because so often, they are told to keep it inside. They are unable to set goals for themselves. They can't accept criticism or feedback. In fact, they don't even want to ask for it. They lose their curiosity and are afraid to speak their mind. We inadvertently do this to our children, when we don't allow the opportunities for them to connect, by doing all things we discuss in this book. It becomes our own fault that our children are not self-aware. So how do we change that? Start by doing all the things talked about in this book, especially in areas of social and emotional development, candid conversations, trying new things, and allowing them to think freely. Make sure you continue to help them identify how they are feeling, and set goals. Most importantly, be the example that you wish to see and take opportunities to reflect with your child as much as possible. Which leads me right into our next point.

Our standards are at an all-time low, in my opinion. Yes, I had to hop right on into it just like that. We accept any and everything as a people, especially in my culture, and communities. Look at our women, look at our men. Look at how we treat each other, and more importantly, look at how we treat ourselves. It is a hot ass mess. Then we treat our children that way and then they grow up to continue to repeat the cycle of lower standards.

I need us to level up more! For ourselves, our communities, our families, and our children. In all actuality for the world! I don't know when quantity became more important than quality, but we need to change that mentality expeditiously. We can't continue to keep accepting just any old thing or settling just for it either. We need to set the standard and be the standard in its entirety, period. This is why raising the standards and values is one of the key jewels I choose to live by in my personal life and business as well. We have to want better for ourselves and be willing to do what it takes to obtain that. If we set a standard for ourselves, our homes, businesses, communities, and so forth, it would be harder to break us and tolerate disrespect. I won't tolerate disrespect, and I refuse to do it to myself. We cannot properly teach children about having standards if we don't have any for ourselves. Remember our children learn more from what we do than what we say. What do your standards say about you?

Lastly, Social Development for children is the ability to form and build relationships not only with their peers but with adults as well. Social Development works a lot in conjunction with emotional development, due to the feelings and emotions they are learning about while encountering these social interactions. There are examples of social development all throughout this entire book. It is good to have your children interact with other children at a young age. It helps them to learn how to work through and develop their social skills. It's a big help in speech development as well. It also teaches and guides them through their emotions. Social Development is critical to the growth and development of a child. It is especially needed right now during a time when we are so disconnected and learning mostly through computers. We are having fewer interactions with humans more and more each day. It's almost as if we are moving into the twilight zone. I don't like it. It really makes me question day to day if I truly know someone. Because a lot of interactions are through the internet. And like I said before, people are crazy! I don't know if I'm getting to know you, or the person you are pretending to be. (Because let's just face it. A lot of people are pretending to be something they aren't.) The internet doesn't feel like a safe place at all, and that is where most of our interactions are happening at the moment. What is this teaching our children about social encounters and interactions? I believe that it is putting out a bunch of false narratives. Because the youth have not been taught to properly process their feelings, they are always in a comparative state. Which has been causing suicide cases to rise, along with what I call Barbie cases. Yes, I said it. People are fake. Fake boobs, fake buts, fake hair, fake nose, fake lips, fake eyes, fake fake fake! Sad to say it's mostly women too. Our children are watching this and seeing this and now wanting to be these images at younger ages! Because the majority of their social interactions are virtual, in virtual reality, you can be whatever you want to be, and not who you truly are. It's not reality, and unfortunately, social media plays a big part in virtual reality, because 75% of it is fake. Yes, that number is based upon an assumption of mine. It may be larger, and honestly, I think it is, but I am choosing to give 25% percent of the people on social media the benefit of the doubt. I know you may be like, well what does all of this have to do with social interactions. EVERYTHING. Children are not seeing other children for who they really are anymore. Or I can say it's becoming less and less, especially with this Covid pandemic. They are stuck in the house or on the computer most of the time. To make it worse the babies 4 and under are just stuck stuck. They are not having playdates or anything if they are not in school. Parents are frustrated and it makes for an insidious situation. Everyone starts to feel trapped and crazy.

Although we are separated most of the time now, from in-person interactions, I believe it is still very important for your children to understand, learn and have those critical social development skills. The lack of social skills could probably cause problems for them in the future. (And I'm treading lightly with that because it's absolutely no telling what the future entails for us now, honestly, I would rather not be a part of Futurama. Unless I get to be like Tris in Divergent. Don't try to box me in haha, but the future seems to be going in more of a Simpsons version type of life… they haven't missed a beat yet DOH!) I watched TV a lot as a child until I went off to college…never really had a TV there. So I like to watch a lot of movies when I want to turn my brain off in case you all were wondering.

Speaking of which, I don't know how many of you guys watch the Big Bang Theory, but it is one of the funniest and smartest shows put together as far as showing very smart individuals who lack social skills. Depicting some of the hardships that they go through in life and in their social and emotional development. Take the time out to watch that show. I'm a weirdo so I like a lot of things that people would consider lame. But that show is definitely funny! I think the world will be full of people like the "geeks" on The Big Bang Theory, along with a whole bunch of Barbies and even some Kens in the future. That is if we don't get a hold of having social interactions away from computers. Especially if we continue to put space in this socializing ordeal. Leaving us with few opportunities to develop our social and emotional skills. People, and how we interact in social aspects, gatherings, and those ordeals, play a big part in our social development, and our children's as well. Although these are my theories and thoughts of what the future will possibly entail, I'm curious to know what others think. Do you think that social interactions and engagements are getting worse? What does the future look like for you? What are your theories about how social engagements of the future will affect our children's social and emotional development?

Chapter T

T *is for*
Thinking skills & Tone

I have been talking about critical thinking skills throughout the entire book. You may not have realized it, but everything beforehand is a part of the process for critical thinking as well. Critical thinking skills are your child's ability to recall, memorize or organize thoughts or make a decision. Ultimately, it is a problem-solving skill. A lot of children are lacking those skills because we are no longer teaching them how to think for themselves. We are no longer teaching them how to figure it out. We are doing it for them or not teaching them anything at all. Now they are just out here. Wondering, making countless harmful mistakes.

Interacting, engaging, having conversations and most importantly asking questions, all of these help with critical thinking. If you are wondering if there are some games you can play to help with the process as well, of course! There are plenty. I'd like you to think of any old school game, and play that with your children. Anything you gotta give directions to. Even puzzles and riddles are all things that can aid in critical thinking skills, and make the exercise of critical thinking fun. As adults, we have to stop and ask ourselves what is it that we truly want our children to learn? What is it that we really want them to be able to fight through and figure out in moments of difficulty? We have to ask ourselves, do we want our children to give up in moments of adversity? Once we have answered all those questions, I think it makes it a little easier for you to allow your children to go through some of those processes alone, to figure things out. It will also make you feel more comfortable in allowing them to speak their mind.

Now, remember, you always have to have some balance in the situation. You gotta know when to step in and when not to. But you're "not to", should be more than you're stepping in. Allow them to do and make the mistakes, but the KEY is to be there to correct them when it happens. Remember not in a negative way! Give the instructions on how to. We have to stop overcomplicating things with them. Just let things be. Leave your biases, traumas, and everything out of it, so you can actually take a look into their mind. You can learn from your children as well. Remember, they're naturally a reflection of you. Make sure you set the proper tone on critical thinking skills and why it is important to have them.

Tone is a big one. I mentioned tone earlier in chapter B, when I talked about tone, and the tone I set in my class. What is tone? Well, MY definition of tone is what you do or don't, will or won't tolerate. The tone is when you have established a clear and concise understanding of the boundaries placed around you. It is also how you are perceived by others because of how you may handle things. Tone has a lot of variables, so I will further explain. At first many may think that I am talking about a sound when referencing tone. That is incorrect. What I want you to do is think of a book you read or a movie you saw. In the beginning, you don't know what to expect. Is it mysterious, scary, or silly? You don't know, but then something happens and bam, all of the sudden the movie gets serious. That seriousness part, that right there, that's the tone. You follow?

I'm not sure if that makes sense to you as I think differently. Every day, in this education life, is a movie, so I thought that would be a great example. It makes perfect sense to me hahaha. But for those of you who it doesn't, let me go even further. See, the tone you set can tell a person whether or not they can try you, majority of the time. Like parents who are actively involved in their child's life. You participate. You ask questions. You're involved. You have set a tone for that teacher. That teacher knows you don't play with your baby and not to try you. They better make sure all their T's are crossed and their I's are dotted. They also tend to appreciate you a little bit more because you communicate all the time and you are active yet you tend to be fair. So as long as no one does anything wrong to your baby, you cool. That's a good tone to set for teachers.

Now, there are other types of tones that parents set for teachers. Parents who come in complaining all the time, yelling at the kids all the time. Got an attitude all the time. You set a tone as well. Your tone says you're hella dramatic. It tells me, let me say what I got to say to get you out of my face and out of my class immediately. Then you got parents who come in talking on the phone, smelling like weed, looking a mess, trying to fight other parents, and teachers. You set a tone as well. I know you may THINK your tone says, don't fuck with me, or I'll beat yo ass, but it doesn't. It's quite the opposite. Your tone says you IGNANT! Yes, I said it .... annnnndddd. You are the parents that I have to say "step into my office" all the damn time!! Whether I'm a teacher, an administrator, or director, y'all be having me get on some real ish with y'all! I be having to stop teachers from wanting to clock out and whoop yo ass. I don't know why y'all be thinking teachers can't fight. Ha! You do know some of us are straight from where you from fam! Calm down. Stop with all that ignant ish! You do know yo baby can attend another school right? Like I be so confused by yall. Try a different tone.

Then we have the parents who are either overbearing or want to make the rules up for the entire class as if they're teaching it. They are the teacher, but they ain't never there. Don't get involved, don't do nothing. Got all the suggestions in the world, but won't come volunteer and see how or why the rules are set up the way they are for your class. You want the whole world to stop what they doing for your one child as if there's not 50 other children in the classroom.

You are anxious and nervous all the time. And guess what, you set a tone as well. It's something in here for everybody! Your tone is stressful. It is stressful as hell! I don't even want your energy near me. I don't even want to talk to you half the time. When you come around, I got to take deep breaths. Put on a fake smile and put on my calming voice. The reason why, is because anything somebody may or may not say to you, you might take the wrong way or out of proportion. You get the "Oh my gosh. Oh my goshing". And the "Well my child needs this, and he shouldn't do that". And "can you check on my child every 5 seconds the air is contaminated it's not good for his soul, he may pass out any moment". Hahahahaha. I'm gonna tell you right now, y'all the type of parents teachers like to send straight to the office. Especially me, cause ain't nobody got time for that! You take all your concerns and your questions to the office because most of the time nothing I say or anybody else will say will be good enough. Half the time, stuff that the office may say won't even be good enough for you type of parents. Lord, when I am the director and I have to talk to you parents, I definitely have to say a little prayer. I'll be like fix it Jesus. Allah, Buddha, whoever. Fix IT!

Short story real quick, for parents like this. I'm trying to understand why if you have all these demands for your child, why they are not homeschooled with the nanny or something. I've had to have these conversations with plenty of parents who think their child is the end all be all in the class. This is my go-to, because it's something I want all my parents to understand. It's my favorite because these parents typically pull this line on me after they ask me and find out I have no children. They be like "Ms. Johnson I don't think you understand". And I be like "I truly do, and I know you think your child is struggling in that manner (whatever manner they seem to make up at the time), but they're truly not". "Please feel free to come and observe anytime without being seen so that you can truly see how your child is engaging and interacting in class. He/she is doing just fine I promise." (They never seem to have time to observe or volunteer which is crazy) "Well Ms. Johnson do you have children?" No ma'am (or sir cause some of you dads be tripp in tripp in too) "Well I don't think that you understand because you don't have children". "Oh, I know this is hard for you and I understand. Your child means everything to you, correct?" "Yes Exactly!" "And I totally get that and understand that, although I may not have any biological children at the moment, when you drop your child off to me I am responsible for their care right?" "Yes correct" "And you would do anything for your child correct?" "Yes". "Do you have more than one?" "Yes I do". "Do you neglect the needs of your other children to focus on one"? "No, I have to address them all". "Exactly". "You are not my only parent Ms. (or Mr.) So and so, I have (however many) children in my class. See your focus is on your child and your child alone. You aren't thinking about the other children. Well, I have no choice. When you and other parents drop your child off to me, I become the parent in your absence. The whole class becomes my babies. And while you are just focused on yours, I have to focus on yours and (however many) in the class. I have to do what's right for ALL my babies and not just one. I'm sure you can understand that, seeing as though you just told me you have more than one child at home, correct?" Shut them up EVERYTIME!!! Teachers feel free to use that one for your overbearing parents! Be prepared for them to try and make your life an absolute living hell afterward though. So stay on top of your p's and q's. Let your work speak for itself and have great relationships with all your other parents. Then they will definitely have no choice but to look like the problem that they are!

Carrying on, I hope this helps y'all understand tone now. I have to deal with all these personalities and tones of the parents as a teacher. As well as the personalities of the children. I, as a good teacher, have to set the tone for my class! Not only for your child but for you the parent as well! This typically gets set in the beginning, as soon as you meet me and I meet my students. Then reiterated a million times throughout the school year. It is backed up by my communications and my expectations for my class. Also, by the way, I treat all individuals in the class fairly. So can you guess which parent tone I am most susceptible to? That's right, the one who is involved, asking questions, communicating, and working with me. Making sure I'm on top of things, following up with me, talking to me about their children. We just be in constant communication. Those are my favorite tone-setting parents. Me setting tones works hand in hand with me setting the standards for my class. It can also work in conjunction with the structure and the routine of my class. For you parents who want me to stop everything and just cater to your child 24/7 365 days a year, that is what tutoring is for. For that one-on-one attention. Also, that's why we rotate centers, but I cannot stop my whole class routine to cater to your child every single day. Especially for stuff that is definitely not life-threatening or not even important. So you stressful tone-setting parents. Keep that in mind.

I urge parents to set more serious and positive tones with their child's teacher and with their children as well. Because the type of tone you set with your children will be relayed over into the classroom too. It can also set a tone on how they will be, or how they are allowed to behave in public or certain situations. I see a lot of these moments become very embarrassing moments for the parents. Therefore I challenge you guys to think about your tone. What does your tone say about you to anybody that you come in contact with? Or what does your tone say for your home?

Chapter U

U *is for*
Understanding

"What I need from you is understannnnndingggggggg. How can we communicate, if you don't hear what I sayyyyyy. What I need from you is understannnnndingggggg, so simple as 1, 2, threeeeeeeee. Understanding is what we need". Yesssssssss, can we say Classic! Where are all of my Escape fans? Did you sing that out loud? We got sing-a-longs in the book too now! U is for understanding. I've already explained in Chapter K how this is something we lack tremendously! It affects our very existence every day. People don't even look for understanding. They just naturally assume. That's the history of the world and the United States. Columbus didn't discover America! Columbus saw something and instead of asking questions, assumed and claimed it. The Pilgrims saw the Native Americans. Instead of looking to understand their ways, they looked to befriend them so they could take them out. "Oh what you doing is soooo different, it must not be right! So let's get rid of them and take over". Let's feast and eat afterward to celebrate! Crazy right?

I explained in chapter K, that we lack an understanding of each other. We also lack understanding of ourselves. We don't take the time to become self-aware or knowledgeable of ourselves. So how do we expect people to search for understanding in, or of others? More importantly, how do we expect to teach the importance of that to our children? Chapter Q showed us how the lack of questioning, can lead to a lack of understanding as well. Not only that, but it seems as if people just don't want you to know, or understand right? We lack understanding of ourselves, other people with different backgrounds and ethnicities, and different cultures and beliefs. There's a lack of willingness to learn more, therefore the opportunity is not often granted to our children. Not gonna stay on understanding too long. But I do want to share something with you. You don't know what you don't know. You won't understand things if you don't take the time to understand. People are joined together by experiences. Including our children! Me being from Chicago and up north, my experiences, my outlook and views on life are completely different from those of my southern counterparts. They think differently, and they act differently. They have different worries and it's because their communities are different. Their families had to grow up in a different atmosphere, the economy is even different around them. I wouldn't understand or wouldn't know that until I put myself into those atmospheres or situations. That is what helps me to have a better understanding of the whys or the hows. We don't do that enough. We don't empathize, along with we don't ask questions or build upon relationships. Not to mention we have big communication problems! How can we understand? Naturally it would be easier for me to understand others who come from big cities, because of the similarities. The same would go in vice versus if I was from down south or an island, and so on. Therefore, I would be more relatable to those individuals. But it takes way more than that to understand. We have to dig deeper. That's part of the whole premise of this book, digging deeper into our relationship with children to understand them better. Also digging deeper with each other as well.

We have the tendency to throw or project our insecurities onto other people, for no reason. It is our way or the highway. I say this a lot. There's more than one way to get to 6. Three plus three isn't the only way. There are a couple of other ways. What we have to figure out amongst each other is why, the way someone chooses to get to the answer 6, is the easiest way for them. Once we have a better understanding, we can now CHOOSE that method as well if and when we see fit. It adds to our knowledge and wisdom. It doesn't take away.

I never understood why, when I saw teachers, or would hear about other teachers going to school, why their professor, internship, practicum, or student teaching teacher would be so gung ho on them teaching in the exact manner as them. First thought that comes to mind every time I experience this is, Thank God my school allowed me to find my teaching voice and MY style. It was encouraged. Yea there were some basics we had to follow, guidelines we had to stay within. But I never had one of my professors or practicum teachers say, "you have to stand like this, talk like this, read like this, do the activity just like that." No. Not ever. Suggestions were made, theories and experiences explained, and questions were answered. All for my understanding to help ME be a better teacher and individual as well.

I want to end with 2 stories. Because I want administrators and directors to stop doing this with your teachers. Assuming and being prejudiced, biased, and acting as if these teachers need you. Because they don't. Most importantly I want you to stop being culturally insensitive. It makes me sick.

Let's start with the story of me working in a kitchen at a particular center in Tennessee. Now I have worked every position in a child care center. Have all the requirements and experience to do so as well. Well, I was the "chef" for this particular school and was in the kitchen working. (If you have not worked in any type of commercialized kitchen, know and understand this, they are loud! The oven, fridge, icemaker, sink, warmers, shit everything makes a noise). Now, for child care, when we prep or prepare food, it is based upon the number of children that are in attendance for that day. Also if you work at a school that does all those special exceptions, you are then required to prepare different food for allergies and preferences. Which is a big ass headache because you really have to be aware of all ingredients in the food. Then don't let you be working for a school that's on the food program, now you gotta do extra paperwork! Anyway, It's a lot of work. Well, imagine being in the kitchen, prepping food, and washing dishes at the same time. You are in the middle of counting, and someone calls, "Ms. Johnson" and you say "huh?!", loudly so they can hear. They say "can you do something"…and you respond "ok". Then the next thing you know, when you go up to do whatever they asked you to do, you're being pulled into the office to address the response. Because why?! They didn't like how you sounded when you responded while you were counting, cooking, and cleaning in a kitchen where you could barely hear. How would that make you feel? As I write this I am rolling my eyes.

Now I gotta ask questions, which is what they should have been doing to gain a better understanding in the first place. "What do you mean you didn't like the way I sounded?" You didn't like the way I sounded busy?!?!? Or that maybe that I can barely hear you?!?!? What do you mean?!? "Well, Ms. So and so (The assistant director who's a white lady) says you sounded like you didn't want to be here. And when you came into work today you weren't acting silly or joking with people. And it did sound like you didn't want to be here when you came through on the intercom". Now I'm laughing because at this point I'm talking to the director who is Black, and knows me. I'm like, "Is that what you believe? Cause at this point I'm so confused. I say, "for one if I didn't want to be here I would say that. You mean to tell me, if I come to work, with a regular face, not mean mugging, not frowning, not smiling. Just looking, that means I don't want to be here? So, if I'm not being super energetic, or silly every single day, that means I don't want to be here? Since when does me just being calm, and chill mean I don't want to be here? Furthermore, y'all didn't like how I sounded on the intercom?

Have y'all been in that kitchen? Do I need to answer like I'm working at Mcdonald's behind the register? Help me understand. It gets busy back there, and sometimes I can't even hear what y'all saying most times, me acknowledging I can hear you was not enough? Do I need to say some other words? I was in the middle of something when y'all called, that doesn't account for anything? How does me saying huh and ok, equates to me not wanting to be here? I didn't huff or puff." I was so confused and beyond irritated because this happens a lot. Someone who doesn't like me or understand the job, can't even get the job done or do it themselves, has to make something out of nothing. I had to tell the director at this point that I didn't appreciate the treatment or the assumptions. A better conversation could have come from this, with the assistant director there, so she could understand me and the kitchen a little better. I also said "when White women make assumptions of my character, without any legitimate reasonings, and without coming to ask me if I am ok? I don't like it and it makes me uncomfortable because now I'm going to naturally think they're on bullshit because that is what typically follows right afterward. Saying something as simple as, "Ms. Johnson, you are usually super energetic, and silly what's going on today? Why so chill?" Would have been so much more valuable or comforting because that would have allowed me to let her know that I am chill more so than I am silly in these places. And since we have only been open for a short period of time, she hasn't been able to experience this part of me yet. That would have led to a better understanding of me and my personality instead of her making assumptions, and then trying to project those assumptions on you. As a member of management, I would have hoped she would have a better understanding of that". Anyway, I don't work there anymore. I got fired later on down the line for I don't know, speaking up for myself. They were literally looking for reasons and ways to get me out because I asked questions and would not let them mistreat me. Not only that, I was educated, so they couldn't just tell me anything. Those stories would be put into another book, along with the others from various other schools. Some of the things that happen are tremendously unbelievable. Can we have a transparent and candid conversation? Open up the door for some more understanding real quick. Remember, "if it don't apply, let it fly". White women directors, assistant directors, women in business or administration. I see this a lot, in every place I have worked at actually, and if not with me, with other Black women. Stop acting as if, when a Black woman doesn't smile, she is angry. I don't know who came up with the terminology, but it's the resting bitch face ok. Or better yet, it's just how we look when we don't smile. Stop trying to make my natural face threatening. WE don't say that about you when you are not smiling. Stop acting as if, when I ask a question, for understanding, I'm being insubordinate or threatening your life. It's a question! For understanding! That's it. We don't do it to you when you have a question. We answer the shit and keep it moving. Stop being scared when we are having a bad day and would just like to be left alone! Nobody is about to whoop yo ass, but you might catch them hands if you keep trying us! We don't do it to you when you are having a bad day, walking around with your snooty attitude, we be like "oh she must be having a bad day", and keep it pushing. We don't take it personally either. We know what you might be upset about, more than likely has nothing to do with us. Therefore, we don't care! But if you want to talk it out, we are here. But don't get that twisted either. Just because you want to tell us all your business does not mean we are going to tell you ours. You wanting to know all of our business, usually leads to it being used against us in some form or fashion later. It never fails! Guess what? We caught on and we just can't have that now can we? More importantly, because I choose not to share my personal business with you, because you like to use it against me, does not make me unapproachable. It doesn't mean I'm not personable either. If a Black woman and dare I say some Black men, don't engage in certain topics with their White counterparts, it's more than likely because you guys are culturally insensitive and we tryna keep the peace in the office because we already sense you don't care and aren't really trying to understand. So just let us be unless you are willing and ready to hear some hard truths. Another thing, it doesn't mean because we work together, that we are now family or friends. We don't take those words lightly. Last but most certainly not least, the most important one of all! When we are tired because we have been doing ALL of the work, we need support. Stop having "anxiety attacks", and stop using your "anxiety" as an excuse not to work. We not tryna hear that bullshit. Get the job done. We don't complain when it's 50 million things on the list we have to do. We don't use the excuse of naturally having PTSD knowingly or unknowingly because of years and years of systematic oppression as an excuse. We get it done! Stop getting mad when we refuse to do your job and our jobs too! And stop tryna say we are not a "Team Player" because we finally speak up and point out what is and isn't being done on your part. It is not my job to do yours! You have no authority over here!!! I don't care what your title is. Especially if you are not leading by example and putting in that work. P.S our little Black babies who are energetic are not bad!!! You can stop watching them as if they are going to pull a knife out of their diaper and kill the other babies. You have Chucky and Jason over there acting a plum fool, but all you can do is concentrate on Daquan. Projecting all this negative behavior on our babies. They are not dangerous!!! Especially at that young of an age! They are babies too! And that's why we check on them and would rather have those little boys and girls in our class and nearby us. Especially our Black Boys. Sincerely A STRONG BLACK WOMAN.

It needed to be said. Because that is why so many child cares and school systems are failing!! Horribly. And this is the other reason why.

One year in Chicago I worked at this center, which had multiple locations which I was to manage. It was in the hood, and it was a small business. Now, this business had a lot of issues that I was hired to resolve. I was required to manage all their sites and train the directors and restructure the operations of the business and everything. Everything that I did I can write another book on, but what I want to focus on are the admin and the teachers. Again, a constant struggle. Tug of war. Teachers were not happy with the administration, and the administration was not happy with the teachers. The first thing I had to do was get to the root cause of the problem. I have a method for this. It's simple really, and it stems from chapter C. Can you guess what it is? In order to make the change, the business owners first have to acknowledge that change has to happen on their ends too. What typically happens in these situations, administrators think they are doing the most for their employees. That the employees should be grateful, and the employees need to step it up, and so on. It becomes a blame game. So to gain understanding I do special surveys. I get the answers, and it totally wakes the business owners up on how their employees actually feel. Almost all the time the owners are in complete shock and total disbelief, and then it turns to anger. Hahaha. I'm laughing, 'cause it's funny. It's funny because a lot of small business owners work from a sense of entitlement, rather than appreciation and that is what eventually sabotages the business. I've done the survey for more than one business and it always helps, and I can't help but picture their faces when I show them the paperwork. It's funny. So the next thing to do, and teachers are not made aware of this yet, but it's to compromise on what to change. Again, that takes the owners accepting and wanting it before we can get to work.

In these moments, teachers ain't believing nothing. Nothing is going to change, therefore you have to make them believe. When this happens, teachers tend to hate me, before they love me. Because they don't understand what's going on, or even believe change is happening. Especially if they don't know you. They don't see the change while they are going through it. I do with them, as I do with my students, parents, and anybody else to be honest. I come in, and set boundaries, rules, and the tone. I come off as an asshole, which I'm totally ok with. Because just like with everyone else, parents, administrators, and students, teachers have a choice. Not only that, my intentions are pure and clear. I truly want the best for everyone and that's what I aim for. The best. Therefore, I'm firm, yet fair. Well first things first, in order to get the teachers to a level where the administration is WILLING to pour into them, I have to show the administration their flaws. It almost always typically stems from a lack of belief in the people they hired in the first place. Ain't that crazy? Especially in education. You don't believe that the people who you hired are capable of getting the job done or even elevating. Unbelievable right? Why hire them then? Oh, I know why. (Rolls eyes).

So I start to pour into the teachers. Speaking their language, putting them up on game, training them, arguing with them, fussing with them, and working with them. Showing more than I am telling. Then attitudes towards me start to change. (I promise everything that I talk about in this book in regards to connecting and bonding, I do with everyone, because we are all learning and growing). Now they are willing to put in the work for me because they see that I am willing to get in the trenches and put in the work for them. Now it's time for me to deliver to them. That means, going back to the owners and saying it's time. I will never forget the day one of the owners came to me and said, "Ms. Johnson, oh my goodness how did you do it? I mean it's running like a well-oiled machine in here. I see these ladies doing things I could never get them to do! And with a more positive attitude too. I see changes in the children, and even the parents! It's crazy they could not stand you when you started and now they love you and have this place operating when you are not here as if you were here. How'd you do it?" I politely said, "aw thanks. I just believed in them, and gave them something to believe in". She looked at me like that's it. And I said, "you can't have poorly trained teachers here and think that they are going to do a superb job. You can't expect a million-dollar service, when you are paying minimum wage, and giving them denigrate vibes. Most importantly if the people who work for you can't see a future for themselves, how are they going to see it for the children they are servicing? You have to be willing to pour into your staff. Me and the staff have an understanding now". As much as I liked being there and working with that center, me and that lady, couldn't see eye to eye on a lot of things. I also have a strong belief in integrity. So eventually me and that center parted ways. I was extremely proud of those girls and what they were able to accomplish and grow through. In their personal struggles and work struggles. I still keep in touch with them, or try to as much as possible.

I see what happened at that center, at a plethora of centers all the time! The administration has a false sense of what is right and what is wrong because they are paying you. But in education, that's just not how this works, because we HAVE to work in unison. One does not work without the other. Without the parents and children, there is no school. Without the teachers, there is no school. Without the school as a whole, there is no opportunity for parents to receive help and teachers to help as many children at one time. I call it the educational circle of life. We have to understand that.

Speaking of the circle of life, that is what understanding does. It connects us to life. Our purpose, our goals, our struggles, our uniqueness, our differences, our alikeness, our cultures, and communities, and more. It connects us to each other, and to the world. Connect being the keyword here. Without understanding, there is no connection. With that being said, are you truly trying to understand your children and students? Do you feel connected? Do your children constantly tell you or others that they feel misunderstood? If so, I would encourage you to work on trying to connect with them a little more, so that you can start to understand them a little better. If we do this more, maybe people would stop looking at differences as such a bad thing. Maybe they will take it for what it is and nothing more. A learning opportunity.

Chapter V

V *is for*
Value & Voice

Value has two meanings. It works hand in hand with the standards and principles you choose to stand behind in life. It also means your worth or the worth of something. I like to think that I am very valuable. In fact, I believe it without a shadow of a doubt. I know when I come around in any shape, form, or fashion that I can add value to a person's life, whether they believe it or not, and I don't have to prove anything to you. All you have to do is sit back and watch. My value grows, the more I grow. The more I learn. The more I believe. You can't put a price tag on me. So don't try.

The other thing that increases my value is the value that I see in others. I'm not talking about the celebrities, superstars, and social media people who blew up. I'm talking about the next-door elderly neighbor who brings popsicles to you on a hot summer day. I'm talking about the young man who gives up his seat on the bus so you can sit down. I'm talking about that neighbor who lets you sit at their house when you're locked out of yours, who calls your parents to let them know what happened and to say that you're okay. I'm talking about that guy in the neighborhood who is taking baby steps to build his business, that gives back to the youth and the community. I'm talking about that mother who is struggling to take care of her four to six kids, but when their friends come over to the house, she feeds them too. I'm talking about YOU! The individual who doesn't have a lot of money in the bank but outchea surviving best they can every day to make it. I'm talking about YOU! If money did not exist, you would still be valuable. Understand that! I can't know it for you. You have to know it for yourself. You have to want it for yourself as well.

The Walking Dead, that is my mother flip in show. I love it. You wanna know why? Because the world is in shambles and it gives this idea of people, and how they act with no government. Most importantly it shows you how they value themselves and how they value others. The best thing about it is Rick's core group. I mean them muthapluckas are survivors, with hearts! At least to me. The series shows their everyday struggle of keeping that heart untainted as best they can. Then when Negan comes, it gives you a different perspective of how everyone thinks they're doing the best thing and what's right for their people. It's deep y'all! Y'all gotta watch it. I can have conversations about the walking dead for hours, but we are going to move along. Anyway, there's a point in the show where Morgan and Rick are talking about the value of people. Their premise is that people are valuable! You can't go around killing everybody, mistreating everybody. If you do, how do you expect the world to sustain and go on? Especially when more than half of it is zombies! Deep right? I told my dad to watch it, he said he didn't need to watch "The Walking Dead" when we are living the show every day. I said, "yea I feel you, it's zombies out here, their bodies just aren't visibly deteriorated". People make the world go round, not money. And if we don't start valuing each other and ourselves, we will essentially be our own detriment. Deep right, haha, a comment from a person who doesn't even like people, right? This is why! Because people are crazy! My Aunt used to say "if you ain't got common sense you ain't got shit". I felt that, and then I met a guy who I would say to all the time "damn bruh you ain't got no common sense"? He would always reply angrily "sense ain't common". I now believe that saying just as much too.

I just don't understand humanity. That's all. What I do understand is we have to do a better job of valuing ourselves first and then valuing each other. Because how can we truly value another person when we don't know our own worth? It is going to be extremely hard for you to see value in someone else when you lack the ability to see it within first. Especially when you care nothing about yourself and don't see the benefit, powers and light you add to the world.

It's time for another story. I was working at this center in Chicago. The center was in the hood. Had very hood parents that did ignant and ignorant shit all the time. Not everyone, but the majority. Well, I guess it was this one parent before I got there who used to just do whatever to whoever they wanted to. At least that's what I was being told. I was told they were an "SP" (special parent), and to just let that parent be. I was like 'yeah, okay". Well as I was making changes to the center, rules and regulations and things, I told them I wasn't letting any SP's slide. Them days were over. It was too much money being written off that we needed in order to make the center better, and if they were scared to talk to the parents, to send them to me. Well, I ended up having to meet with a lot of parents. Basically, I stood my ground, offering payment plans or offering them the chance to leave. I had to explain to them that we are no longer conducting business the old way. If they didn't like it, that's fine. They could leave and I would help them find another place suitable for their needs. But if they chose to stay, it was certain standards that they would have to uphold. Do you know what happened? That's right. All that damn foolishness stopped. The owners, the director, the "billing department", and teachers, could not believe it. Those parents (at the worst location) did not dare disrespect me. For a moment they did try the teachers, director, and the "billing department" at times. I always had to step in to stop that disrespect too. "You are not allowed to disrespect anyone caring for your children. You don't like it here, no one is holding you hostage". All that shit ceased! Later on in the year that one special parent everyone warned me about went through a certain situation that I'm not going to go into details about for the sake of that parent's privacy, because the shit was all over the news. Both incidents. They ended up getting kicked out of their home, and the parent came to talk to me. Now by this time, the parent had been caught up on payments and was acting right, being respectful and everything. So when we heard about what was going on with that family, I was preparing for a setback. So when they came and talked to me, the parent let me know that they were kicked out of their home, and we're looking for a job and somewhere to stay. I got with the billing department, talked to them about the situation, and arranged the payments. We also worked to help that parent find shelter because they were looking for a job, and had some other issues, which caused the children to need a safe place. So I told the parent although we were full, they could come to the center after school. I then came up with a plan and let the owners know, because technically if the state came in on the right day we would have gotten in trouble if we got caught. (That conversation was a situation in itself, I'll shed light on that conversation later) But that was something I was willing to risk to help this parent out.

One day something happened and the parent was sent to me while I was working at another location. The parent looked tired and off. I had the parent step into the storage closet with me because it was no other place for privacy. (Yes I said closet, and I let everyone know to knock on the door if they needed me). While in the closet, I sat on a box and told the parent to talk. The parent didn't want to talk because they were angry, and they were worried I'd get mad at them. So I said, "(Name) if you don't say what you need to say get that shit off your chest!" So the parent started crying and talking and cursing. They were mad. The parent was mad at their child, blaming the child for everything. I did nothing but listen. When the parent was done, they were shaking and quiet. I asked if they were finished. They just said, "I don't know what to do". I asked for permission to keep it real with them and just be honest. The parent was like "gone head, Ms. Johnson". I'm laughing to myself right now because I can still hear and picture the way they said it. I knew they didn't want to hear anything, but, since they gave me permission, they were gone hear it anyway. I told the parent, they needed a therapist. I was worried about the things the parent was saying because it sounded as if the parent was going to harm their child because they were so angry. I then told the parent they couldn't get mad at the child for what the child was doing because the child learned it from somewhere. What was the parent doing to set a better example for their children? I said, "You upset about the fighting but before I came here, you were up here fighting, trying to fight teachers. Every day cussing out people who care for your children". I told the parent what they was gone do, which was sit there in the closet with me. Cry, curse, yell, scream. Get it all out and then go out there and be better for their children. Better for themselves, and know that I will help in any way I could. But the parent had to want it for themselves. I didn't want them to take their frustrations out on the children, so I told them to take it out on me. I told them "this may be a blessing in disguise for you. A wake-up call because I believe all the trouble that the older child was getting into was a cry for help, and you were not listening. Now God made it so that you have no choice but to listen". The parent started hitting their hands. I'm like, "let it out". They was like "I just want to scream". I said "go ahead, scream. No one can hear what's going on up in here. They be screaming out there all the time anyway". So the parent yelled and started to cry, saying things angrily. I then went over and I hugged that parent and just held the parent and let them cry on my shoulders. When they finally calmed down, I asked if they were okay, and they said yeah. I said, "okay, go find a job. Get your mind right". I said I was going to look up some professional people they could talk to and I wanted them to talk to them. They were like "okay", we left the closet and they said thank you and apologized. I told them they had no reason to apologize. They needed to get that out, and anytime they wanted to talk, let me know. A week later, they were in a happier space. They were talking to a counselor and were in the shelter.

One day because we were getting rid of milk that we could not keep. That parent was coming to pick up some milk that day. When they saw me they told me "come outside Ms. Johnson. I want you to meet somebody". I can't remember who the lady was I was introduced to at the time. But the parent was excited and told me that they got a job and some people were trying to help them get a house. Then the parent introduced me to the lady in the car. Then told the lady in the car, I was Ms. Johnson, and that they loved and appreciated me. The parent was so happy. The parent said, "Ms. Johnson give me a hug". I gave them a hug and they said thank you. I was so happy for them. So excited to see that parent in a happy space.

I didn't see the parent too much after that because I wasn't there too much longer. I often checked on them through the teachers. I told the teachers that if that parent ever needed my number to give it to them. This story means a lot to me because during this trying time for that parent, one of the owners wanted to kick this parent out. So imagine how that conversation went when I told them that I told this parent their children could come after school, at no cost, because they needed a safe place. One of the ladies said to me "well you wanted to kick them out in the beginning"! I said, "I was willing to kick anyone out at the beginning that was not ok with the new changes. That was also because of what y'all were talking about as far as the behavior and payment before they held up their end of the bargain when changes were made. I haven't had a problem with them after that. I had told them this is not the time to turn our backs on someone when they truly need our help. You don't do that. You always talking about "the babies, the babies", and "Ms. Johnson think about the children. Well that's what I was doing. I was thinking about the children". That was my argument. So that was the conversation that took place behind the scenes when I originally told the parent what I would do for them. The parent didn't know I was going hard for them. They didn't even know they were this close to being kicked out during a super hard time. These are the types of things that people don't see or even know that are going on half the time. That moment of support did more good than anything, and I was extremely happy it didn't go to waste, cause bae bae!!! I would have been chewed out too much if that opportunity was taken for granted by that parent.

A year later. One of the old teachers from the center got in contact with me. We caught up, and she told me something that I didn't know and it meant a lot for me to hear. She said, "you know such and such and so so, my old student parent?" I was like "yea, how they doing?" She said "Oh they doing so good. I saw the place they live in, they live over west now. They like their job and the children are doing so much better. Praise God! The relationship with the older child has gotten much better". I was like "really?!!" She said "yeah, I can't believe how much they turned their life around". I was like "that's great". She continues to say "you know how much that parent loved you?" I was like, "naw not really". She continued saying, "They used to come to my class and talk about you all the time". I was like "really I didn't know that". She was like "yeah, they used to come in at first asking who you were and who you thought you were. I would tell them you were here to help. Then later on they would come in and be like, "you know Ms. Johnson don't play, let me make sure I have my little payment ready. I don't want her kicking me out". I was cracking up. She continued the story saying, "they would sit there and tell me how they could give Ms so and so and Ms. such and such a sob story and they will wipe their bill away. Then she says that parent was like, "Nah, baby, not Ms. Johnson. Ms. Johnson be like I ain't trying to hear that ish". I was dying laughing. I said "they used to tell you all that"?! She was like yeah, I said "See, that's why I don't be playing with these parents. These parents will try to get over on you if you let them. They just like these damn kids!" We laugh and she asked "is it true that you talked with them in a closet Ms. Johnson?" And I was like "yeah". She was like "I ain't believe it when they told me, I'm like a closet?!" I cracked up laughing. I said, "I was at the other location and the office had too many ears, and the after-school room had the children in it. The storage closet was big enough for us to sit and have a conversation. I could tell they needed to talk and I ain't want everybody in their business. Plus I could tell if someone said the wrong thing to them that day, they may have went off and exploded. I ain't feel like breaking up no fights. It was during the time when all that stuff was going on, and they were on the news, and people were whispering having stuff to say. You know how that go. So I was like "step into this closet." It wasn't a small closet!" and we started laughing. She was like "ok, that sound more like you, I wasn't sure. Honey, I don't know what you said to them in that closet but it worked. They would come and talk to me about being better, for their children. When they told me that, I was like, Praise God! They said, "Ms. Johnson made me see some things in that closet that day". That's all they said, I was confused like closet?!" Hahaha. They said when they talked to you, it was like someone was seeing them for the first time in life. They said they never had anyone just listen to them in that manner and be that kind to them before. They said you weren't even mad, and they felt like you truly cared and that they mattered". I was like "they do and I needed them to see it for them self though". She was like "Yes child and I'm happy too, cause honey I used to have to say many prayers for those children cause baby you should have seen how they used to be before you came. Off the chain! When Ms. Such and such was the director, they used to go at it! Do you hear me? It would be unbelievable!" I said, "I could believe it. They tolerated it". She said "I could have never guessed that that parent would have did a 360 with you". I said "I don't know about all that". She said "Ms. Johnson I would never forget the first time we had a meeting and you talked to us alone at the center and the teachers kept coming to me complaining about you. I had to always tell them, give her a chance". I was like "awwwwww thank you. I didn't know that either". She was like "yeah, cause when you told everybody that you not playing with these parents you would fight these jokers if they came in here with the Ra Ra"… At this point, I'm crying laughing on the phone, I was like "I was dead serious", she was like "I know!" She was like "but you didn't have to, but that's what holding these parents accountable do, it changes things. The teachers, we hadn't had anyone stand up for us like that either. So that's when they started to believe. Because Ms. Such and such already told me you were coming before you got there. I knew what you were there for. You made a world of a difference and I'm glad". I said "awwwww thank you", and we started talking about some other things.

For me, it wasn't merely just the fact of holding them accountable. The neighborhood I worked in did not see their value. They did not see their children's value, the teachers' value, or the center's value. That was something I wanted to change. So I started by setting standards. I completed it by not allowing them to devalue me, the center, the children, the teachers, and most importantly, themselves. They had a choice ultimately remember? Stay and get with the program or leave. We have the power to be better if we truly want to be. We can not be to our children in which we are not to ourselves first. So value yourself, and your children. It makes a difference. That leads us to our next V-word.

Voice. You have been hearing me talk about not taking your child's voice away this whole entire book. Therefore, I'm not going to stay here long. Because hopefully by now you understand. I just want to encourage you to let them have a voice. This allows you to get to know your children better. Understand them better. It also increases their confidence. It can even lead to them being a voice for others as well if they choose. Throughout history, that is one thing that we have always been creative in doing, no matter how much an individual has tried to take our voice away. We still found a way to make our voices be heard. So I say to you, encourage your children to speak up, encourage them to talk to you, and say what is truly on their minds. Encourage them to stand for what they believe in. Encourage them to speak their truth! Our voices are powerful beyond measure and our wildest imaginations! Yet, you will never know it until you use it. Do not intentionally do to your children what people have been trying to do to us for years.

Chapter W

W *is for*
Willingness

W is for willingness. This is also something that I have mentioned several times throughout this book. We want to keep that fire burning in our children that keeps them wanting to learn. Now you have tons of creative ideas and ways to do so given to you in this book. I challenge you to get creative every day to keep it going. It is our willingness to do, that keeps us moving forward. If you are unwilling, then nothing will change and nothing will grow. You will be left at your last "growth spot". Look at it like height. If you stop growing at 4 feet 5 inches, that is how tall you will be for life. The same goes for your mind. If you stopped learning at a certain point and are not willing to continue to learn and be better, that version of you will be your latest, but not your greatest version. Eventually in some manner children start to be a reflection of us. Let them see your willingness to learn, grow, play, and try new things. Step out of your comfort zone and be you! Let them see that while also doing all of the other things we have discussed in this book. Keep that fire ablaze so that children can still want to learn. If they are uninterested, they are unwilling. Help them to keep that eagerness to learn and grow, that's all I'm asking.

Chapter X

X *is for*
Xcuses

X is for xcuses. Yes, it is spelled wrong intentionally. I don't feel like reading the dictionary to find an x word in relation to connecting and bonding with individuals. So shoot me! If you come up with one, let me know. I love learning too. The X also serves as a play on words because I want y'all to put an X over everything keeping you from change and growth! Put an X over everything that needs to get the boot. Whether it's your eating habits, communication style, your lack of interest or willingness to grow. Throw that out the window today. Let's eliminate the excuses! Choose to be better, to have better relationships with each other, and more importantly, our children. If this book has taught you nothing but "I can do better with my communication with my children", I am a happy camper. Now, of course I'm joking. If you believe that, you crazy! This book should have taught you more than that. For one, it should have given parents a look into teachers and their struggles, and vice versa. It should have shown how we essentially need each other and should have mutual respect and understanding for one another. It should show you how the school systems are really jacked up yes, but can also play a critical role in being a safe haven as well. It should have taught you how to pay attention, ask questions, get involved, be more understanding, and ultimately eliminate the excuses as to why it can't be done and figure it out. Figure out how to make it happen. How to work with your children, how to be there for them, and more importantly, know that it is no one else's responsibility to do so but yours. Remember, I and other teachers out here, are momentary. We can quit our jobs at any time, and as you can see, more elements go into that why. The children are usually the last reason. We are humans too. We have lives too. But you as the parent, are teachers forever, and ever, ever and ever, ever. So step it up. Be better. Be better to your children. Be better teachers, to your children. Your best and most important classroom will always be at home, no matter what. Be better. Not for me or anyone else but for yourself, your children, and simply because the world just needs better people in general. Let's eliminate the excuses people. Choose to be better.

Chapter Y

Y *is for*
Yes

Y is for yes. Yes, we can like Obama and them said! Yes, we can be better. Start saying yes, to push yourself to be better. Start saying yes to getting out of your comfort zone. Start saying yes to trying new things. Start saying yes to meeting new people. Start saying yes to learning about different cultures. Start saying yes to loving yourself. Start saying yes to getting to know yourself. Start saying yes to new experiences. Once you start saying yes to yourself and giving yourself the love, care, and above all treatment it deserves, you can start saying yes to your children's growth and development in a healthier, less traumatic, and more supportive way. Say yes, I can do this. Yes, I can do it. Yes, I could play this game with my child. Yes, I could do this activity with my child. Yes, I can sit here and talk to my child about their day. Yes, I can motivate my child to be better and give them encouraging words. Yes, I can show them how to do things the correct way. Yes, I can take on their interests, and spend more time with them. You will start saying yes to them in a more loving way, with a new attitude and a new perspective. You will start saying yes you can do this because you're telling yourself yes, I can do it. Cut the negativity out. Stop telling yourself what you can't do. What you ain't gonna do and what you don't do. Stop stunting you and your child's growth. Do it. Even if you have to take baby steps in doing it. In no way is this a contradiction to everything discussed in chapter N. This is you saying yes to self-love. Any and everything that will help you become more aware, positive, and comfortable in your own skin, mind, and beauty of and for yourself. Not materialistic things that don't matter. Enhance and work on your weaknesses to turn them into strengths. Say yes to being better. Say yes to growth. Say yes to an overall healthy mind, body, and spirit, for you and your child.

Chapter Z

Z *is for*
Zen

Last but not least, Z. Z is for Zen. What Big Sean say? Zen the fuck out. And yes Zen is a real word. It is an act of meditation and intuition leading you to a peaceful state. We have to learn how to calm the spirit, mind, and body. It is good for the soul. We spew so much hatred and confusion out onto one another, that we don't know what peace feels like or looks like. It always amazes me when some men be like, "be my peace." "I want peace." "Don't disturb my peace." As if they are the only ones who deserve or want it. Y'all do know women want it too right? I believe when we want peace, we must be that for ourselves first before we can be it for each other. You can't want all this peace, but don't know how to be at peace. You create all this havoc and then be talking about you want peace or someone has to be your peace. Don't think I'm coming down on just the men, because this goes for women too. The bible has already told us that there is nothing worse in the world than an odious woman. Ultimately the question becomes do you know how to be at peace? Or create a peaceful state for yourself and your children?

Children need to learn how to be at peace as well. How do we be at peace with our minds and body? How do we calm down? This is extremely important for active children, and children with behavioral issues to learn. It will take tons and tons of practice, and time as well. What we like to do in early childhood education is start with breathing. We do a lot of breathing exercises, taking deep breaths, inhaling, and exhaling, but it doesn't have to stop there. What people don't know is peace doesn't only have to come with meditating in breathing to calm the mind or the body. You don't necessarily have to sit in the 'crisscross applesauce' position all the time and take deep breaths to be still. I like to think it is something that comes easily and naturally for you to do as well.

For instance, for me, when I was younger it was art and poetry that calmed my soul. A diary as well (but that became a headache because my sisters always wanted to read my diary, so it became less peaceful. Poetry though, they didn't want to read that Ha!) It helped me collect my thoughts and somewhere along the lines, I got away from that. That's probably why after college in pursuit of my dreams, I was a lot more angrier and stressed out. I wasn't doing things that were natural outlets for me anymore like art, poetry, dancing, and sometimes not even listening to music. I was all over the place. It was crazy. I was focusing on everyone else, trying to help everyone else except myself. I noticed that, although college was a lot, I was still at peace with myself because I was focusing on no one but me at the time. Afterward, I wasn't doing those things anymore.

My family and friends notice that when I paint now, (I don't do it as much as I used to when I was younger), I kinda zone out. My friends laugh at me and say I get real serious. And it's not that I get real serious, it's just that it soothes me. I'm not thinking of anything else when I'm doing it. It clears my mind. Reading does the same thing except it takes my mind away from what is currently going on at the moment. They used to have this saying when I was younger if you wanted to travel read a book. Most of the time that's what my mind does while reading, it travels. I had fallen off of that for a while too.

As I got older what brought me peace became me driving on an empty road. My family and friends be like, "you be driving everywhere". I'm like "yea, I like to travel and sightsee", it clears my mind every time. I actually like driving and still do that a lot till this day. The next thing is taking a shower bath. Yes, I said shower bath. I like sitting in water while more water runs down my body. Call me weird if you want, but I like it. You should try it sometime. I can't take bubble baths anymore. I remember full-fledge crying when I found out in college y'all, like full-fledge tears while in the hospital! I can laugh about it now, but it broke my heart then. The doctors were looking at me like, is she serious? But that's how serious baths were a form of peace for me and I was like noooooooo. I thought taking baths would never be the same without bubbles hahahaha. I later came to peace with just sitting in regular bath water with the shower running on me. Ha!

I am completely okay with sitting and being alone. Sitting with my thoughts. I actually do that a lot, maybe too much. When I need to turn my mind off, that is the main time I turn the TV on. When my mind is just going at a million miles per hour because I got so much going on, that is how I tune my thoughts out. Momentarily though, because if I don't figure my way out of a situation that will drive me crazy as well. But I try my best to be cognizant of that. What drains my energy and stresses me out the most is people. I work and socialize with people all the time and it is very nerve-wracking sometimes. Yes. I like to and can have fun with people. I will turn up with certain people all the time! I like to play and joke around with certain people as well. It's fun. Smiling and laughing is good for the soul. But unfortunately, when working in the public sector, those are not the people you run into. It's the people who like to fight, blame, and complain all day! Especially complain! Lawd! Then they don't know how to talk to you or have a conversation. Man, it can start to harden your heart. You can start to not care, and say fuck these people. I know I went through moments like this several times. I'm telling y'all, I'm definitely not leaning into my own understanding nor strength when working with the public sector. While also trying to remain sane, keep a positive attitude and keep my peace, there have been several times in my life when I have gotten depressed. Even tried to fool myself into giving up. Like fuck all this! Short story alert!

When I say giving up, I mean working with children and people. Not suicide. Although when I was nine and my mom was going through all of what she was going through, I was so sad, that I told my brother that I wanted to die. (I'm not even sure if he remembers this). He told me not to ever think like that again, and he bet not hear me talk like that again either. He was so serious, and because I loved, admired, and respected my brother so much when I was little, I never did. My brother doesn't know but he saved my mentality a lot when we were younger. I also had a mental breakdown when I found out what Sickle Cell really was in high school. All that time I just knew it hurt. That was my definition of Sickle Cell. My body hurts. I was so sad and depressed one-day freshman year, caught walking home, he saw me and was like "what's wrong". I was like "I'm going to die". I laugh as I write this because just writing this out shows me an even bigger correlation. He laughed a little and said "what?!" I said, "I'm not gone live past the age of 21, I may not make it to see that age". He said, "what the hell are you talking about Meka". I replied, "I saw it in Biology today! They said people with Sickle Cell don't live past the age of 21 on the tape". He said "Oh girl, you know how old that tape is? It's dated, that's not true. Medicine has been updated and science is better now. Besides they told mama when you were born that you would not make it past the age of 12. You still here ain't you?" I cheered up and said "Yeah"! He was like, "so you have purpose and that's why you still here. You not going nowhere no time soon". And just like that, I was happy! I also learned a new word, Purpose, and walked around with new confidence of not leaving this earth until it was fulfilled. Ironically later on while growing up and going through high school, my purpose was made more clear to me.

I would often pray when my mom got sick to God, to not let me die of Sickle Cell or from a gunshot. (We lived right down the street from Jackson Park Hospital, that's all I heard, it felt like damn near every night, gunshots and the ambulance). I would tell God that if I had to die, it should be in my sleep when I was old. So seeing that video in high school really did something to me. It disturbed my peace. I was messed up that whole entire day until I got home, and ran into my brother. So essentially my brother stopped me from thinking about death twice, restored in me my value, and reassured me that I would not leave this earth until my purpose is fulfilled. That is what ironically, makes me not afraid to die till this day. Because I now believe that if I die, I have fulfilled my purpose on earth. Anyway, back to the people.

So yes, there have been times when I have tried to fool myself into thinking that maybe I'm not supposed to work with children or make a better place for them. I literally would stop trying to work along those lines, and would be even more miserable y'all I swear. I kept coming back to it, someway, somehow. So I had to figure out how to create peace for myself amongst the chaos. Because I am so passionate about working with children, I had to learn how to balance. And y'all when my balance is offffff, I'm a biiiiittttchhhhh. Yes. That's the hard part about working in the social sector. Balancing. Caring enough in ways that you don't hinder the people who you are trying to help, yet not caring enough to ensure that you don't start to hinder yourself, your family, or your goals. Mannnnnn say that ain't the balancing act that all people who work with other people don't struggle with, in maintaining their peace! It is a hard thing to do! And sometimes you get knocked off your game, but like Beyonce said, you gotta find your way back! Beyonce said it so you gotta do it now... Therefore, when I deal with the public all day, there's nothing better than a couch and a bottle of wine, if I got it. Do you hear me?!? I just want to sit and lay!! I have to calm my mind mostly in these moments, and my body because I'm very active. I have to refocus myself. So when I sit myself down, bet not nobody say nothing to me! Give me a moment, some wine, and maybe some tunes, but shhhhhhhhh. Let me just be for a moment.

When I'm working with children, and I want to create calm moments with them, it's lights off. I typically like sitting in the room with natural light only. So it works out perfectly for me when we turn the lights off and let all the natural light in. We sit crisscross applesauce, taking deep breaths, and a lot of times I have us close our eyes. Except me, I be peeking, gotta keep one eye on the kiddos at all times. We talk in whispers, and we move around lightly. Depending on the day, if it's a very stressful day, the lights stay off the whole entire day. We do fun activities, with the lights off. Glow-in-the-dark activities while allowing only natural light in. We have conversations about the sun and nature. If it was up to me I would pick natural lights over light bulbs any day. I'm not sure why, but there is just something about natural light and the sun beaming in through the window. It's serene.

When the children are upset, we give them space. We oftentimes have spaces that we create in the classroom called Safe Spaces. When the children need a moment to calm down or have a tantrum, or whatever, that is where they go. But if you don't have safe spaces in your classroom, the library doubles as that space. But if you got 20-something kids in your classroom, when you break out into centers, that space is usually full. Usually, if the child has a moment and needs to calm down I like to let them do what it is they like to do the most. It could be puzzles, art, or anything. Sometimes it's just them wanting to sit right next to me and watch everything I do. And I am totally ok with that if it'll stop you from trying to beat up the next child. I encourage you all to observe your children in moments of tranquility. What brings them peace, or to a calmer state? And you bet not say no dang on iPad either! Find out what gets them to really just chill and relax. Build upon that for moments of Zen.

What brings you the adult to a peaceful state? We oftentimes have to calm ourselves, for our children's sake. You know, things like postpartum depression and those ordeals are real. We often in early childhood education have to tell parents when they have newborns to create a safe word in times when they just feel like they are about to break. Something they could say or tell to a loved one, which means I am in desperate need of help, or a moment to myself. This is created so another person can know how and when to step in and help take the load off, or take you to a psychiatrist. What do you do to calm your nerves and still keep that balance for yourself? Hell, we as teachers, oftentimes have to do it for one another. I gave you a brief example of it in chapter E. Although I do think the teachers could have done a better job of working with the student, they said that safe phrase! Hey, "I'mma bout to lose it"! Don't think that teachers don't have those moments because they are trained to deal with them. If you can't handle one crying infant, can you imagine how a teacher feels about handling 4 to 8? There's moments when we need to step out, calm down and recollect too. We have to have those Zen moments, those safe moments, and those safe words because sometimes dealing with a lot of children at one time could be overwhelming. Especially when there is no support from the administration. So for those of you that have one child and are being driven crazy. Imagine a teacher with 10, 20, 30, 40 of those children in one class at one time. A class that probably isn't even big enough! We have to breathe!! Do you hear me?!

All in all, we have to know what brings us to a peaceful state. What clears our minds and what makes us smile? What enhances our spirits? We have to do more of that. We must create a lot more of those spaces for ourselves, and our families. With that being said, I want to end the ABCs by encouraging you to create and learn more about how to create those moments for yourself. Hear me when I say this, chill out, everything is going to be okay.

Word From The Author

I want to thank everyone for taking the time to read the book. I hope that you gained a lot of knowledge from this and feel like you have a better understanding on how to create those moments of connectivity so that your bond with your children can be stronger. And not just children either. Understand we are not perfect, but we are all worth more. But it takes us knowing that for ourselves before we can know it for anyone else. Even these tiny, beautifully made creatures we call babies. I promise if you start to do some of these things with your children and students, you will start to see a change within the first month. You must stay consistent though.

This book is dedicated to anyone who ever felt disconnected from themselves or others. This is dedicated to teachers and all those who are working with children on an everyday basis and feel like their voice isn't being heard. Who feels like it doesn't matter what they say or do. Who feels unappreciated. Let me say to you that it does matter! And keep doing it. Stand your ground, be unapologetically you, especially when your results in education speak for itself! If no one has said it to you, let me be first to say Thank you, I'm proud of you and everything that you accomplish with these children! You think the children are not paying attention and the parents don't care, they do! You may not hear all the praise they have for you, but trust me they are telling somebody.

This is for the schools that dare to set themselves apart and do what's right for the children. You are going against all the grains! And although the school systems are being grouped together because of a bunch of bad apples, understand parents see the difference in your school. Continue to keep that uniqueness about yourself. Continue to understand that there are a lot of things that can be done differently with the education system and continue to work on that because it's needed. We will need more, and we can't accomplish that change alone.

This is for the parents who are doing their best. We see you, we acknowledge you! Keep it up. Parenting, like teaching, is not a "one size fit all". You have to get creative often, and do what is right for you and your family, making tough decisions and sacrifices daily! We know that. Don't think we don't. That's why there are many organizations and people out here doing everything they can to help you out! I urge you to not let that help become a hindrance. If no one has ever told you, let me be the first to say to you as well, Thank you! And YOU GOT THIS! Keep pushing forward, learning, growing, and focusing! Your babies are watching!

This is for all those who are working in the social sector, especially with children! Let us pray. God continue to protect our heart, guide our feet, wash our heart, order our steps, protect our minds, guide our tongues and grant us balance and peace. Let the social sector say Amen! Ha!

This book is dedicated to ALL my teachers who believed in me! Saw things in me that I didn't see in myself. Who would check on me and see how I was doing. Who respected my stubbornness (Shout out to LU) when I refused to sit down somewhere because I was sick or in pain. Who challenged me to be better and aim higher, even when I didn't know what the hell you were talking about at that moment. For cursing me out and making me take on more responsibilities and forcing me out of my comfort zone. Constantly! Even tho y'all knew y'all was getting on my nerves hahaha. For making me think. For boosting my confidence. For going above and beyond when you didn't have to! For making me stand up in front of the class and talk, showing me how to make my nervousness work for me. For ALWAYS allowing me to be myself no matter what!!! And for every single teacher who always told me I would make a great author because of the papers I've written. For saying my storytelling style was very unique. For encouraging me to write a book, way before I started investing in myself and hearing it over and over again from other people. Well, I finally did it! I hope you like it! Thank you for being the first to believe that I could.

This book is dedicated to my friends who have supported me from near or from afar. Whether I talk to you every day or once in a blue moon. Thanks for keeping me grounded. Talking some sense into me when I'm about to explode. Being a shoulder I can cry and lean on. Believing in me when it seemed no one else did. Helping me even when I didn't want it, or when I refused to ask. For cursing me out and holding me accountable. For being more than a friend, for becoming family. We get on each other's nerves too, sometimes. But at least I know you will curse my ass out if I need it HA! You won't allow me to waddle in self-pity for long. Y'all gone tell me what I need to hear, and not what I want to hear! I love yall. Thank you!

Last but not least this book is dedicated to my family! No matter how dysfunctional we may be, ahaha. No matter how many fights we have had. No matter how many disagreements and so on and so forth, and I'm talking to MY ENTIRE family not just the immediate, I love y'all. I'm proud of y'all. I appreciate y'all. We had tough childhoods. But we made it through. There are so many more stories I could have put in this book in relation to family (especially mine) and the education system. But I didn't. Whether you know it or not, or believe it or not. You all have inspired me to be better, in some way, shape, form, or fashion. You are all a part of the reason I am the way I am today. And when you tell yourself I get on your nerves, understand, it's your fault! Hahahaha. Because part of you is in me, in some way, shape, form, or fashion! It is my family that made me believe in my power. Whether directly or indirectly. We are strong and resilient. And don't ever think otherwise. And know that I go hard on y'all just like I do with

189

everything, and everyone else. If not more. It's because I sincerely love you to death! No matter how much you irk me. My family has always been my biggest challenge with balance and peace. Cause y'all are the craziest ones of all! Hahahaha! But you are also the funnest, yea I said it, the funnest too! In my journey I haven't opened up to y'all as much, I just started 4 years ago, and that was because it was part of the process. And it needed to be done. And I know a lot mentioned in this book may come as a surprise!! So, SURPRISE!!! Yea I said it! I felt it, that happened, and I'm still here! Just know that I love you! And y'all better hope I don't write any more books. Hahaha! I might need to, we would definitely be trillionaires! Ha!! They didn't even hear all the good stuff! HA!

In short to the public, I too still work on strengthening connections with my family every day. I want y'all to know that nothing I have said in this book has, and does not go unpracticed for myself. I see the changes needed in everything for me as well. Not just in the education I provide, but the education, knowledge, and wisdom I put into practice for myself every day too. Know, that it will continue forever. Because strengthening bonds is a lifetime ordeal. It will continue to be needed as you go, and as you grow.

In conclusion, know that we won't be able to work with one another, build with one another, take care of one another, and so on if we don't strengthen our bonds with one another. Let alone our children. Yes, it takes a village to raise a child, so why don't we have them? We don't communicate with or get to know one another enough, let alone the children we care for. This is essentially why our villages are no more. I hope that sharing these real scenarios and real experiences, helps you to understand why having villages is so important and how they help us all.

Families, we must do better. Schools, we must do better. Teachers, we must do better. In order to do better, we must work together! Because the reality of the situation is one does not work without the other. We need each other, and all of it starts with us building, growing, learning, and working together. Remember, our children are watching and learning from us. We need to unify once more to save our communities, children, and families. Tell me, when it comes to making a difference with your children, what are you fighting for?